Thanks to my brilliant editor Emma Dods, to the team at Farshore, to the generous and inspiring contributors, and to everyone who loved *Why Money Matters* and spurred me on to write my second book. D.M.

First published in Great Britain in 2024 by Red Shed, part of Farshore

An imprint of HarperCollins*Publishers*
1 London Bridge Street, London SE1 9GF
www.farshore.co.uk

HarperCollinsPublishers
Macken House, 39/40 Mayor Street Upper
Dublin 1, D01 C9W8

Red Shed is a registered trademark of HarperCollins*Publishers* Ltd.

Text © Deborah Meaden 2024
Deborah Meaden has asserted her moral rights.
Illustrations © HarperCollins*Publishers* 2024
Cover typography illustrated by Thy Bui.
Cover photograph of Deborah Meaden by Charles Glover.

With thanks to Sophie Ellis-Bextor, Gary Neville, Steven Bartlett, Joe Lycett, Tanya Steele, Anusha Shah, Andy Jefferies and Beth Chilton.

ISBN 978 0 00 865152 7
Printed and bound in the UK using 100% Renewable Electricity at CPI Group (UK) Ltd.
003

A CIP catalogue record for this title is available from the British Library.

Stay safe online. Any website addresses listed in this book are correct at the time of going to print. However, Farshore is not responsible for content hosted by third parties. Please be aware that online content can be subject to change and websites can contain content that is unsuitable for children. We advise that all children are supervised when using the internet.

Disclaimer: Every effort has been made to ensure that the information in this book is accurate at the time of going to print. The information in this book is for general guidance and educational purposes only. It is not a source of financial or legal advice. In addition, neither HarperCollins nor the Author offer investment advice and all financial investments carry risk. You should therefore also seek independent financial advice before making any investment. HarperCollins and the Author make no guarantee of positive financial results by using the methods illustrated in this book.

MIX
Paper | Supporting responsible forestry
FSC™ C007454
www.fsc.org

This book contains FSC™ certified paper and other controlled sources to ensure responsible forest management.

For more information visit: www.harpercollins.co.uk/green

# DEBORAH MEADEN
# TALKS
# MONEY

RED SHED

# CONTENTS

**CHAPTER 1:**
**MONEY MAKES THE WORLD GO ROUND**
9

**CHAPTER 2:**
**EARNING MONEY**
31

**CHAPTER 3:**
**SAVING MONEY**
57

**CHAPTER 4:**
**SPENDING MONEY**
85

**CHAPTER 5:**
**BORROWING MONEY**
113

**CHAPTER 6:**
**STARTING YOUR OWN BUSINESS**
125

**INDEX**
142

# INTRODUCTION

Money is such a huge part of our lives, so learning how to make it work best for YOU is important. That's why I wanted to write this book!

From when I was young, my family would talk about how to have enough money to do the things we wanted to do (not ALL the things, just the ones that really mattered to us!). I think chatting over the table about ideas was how I started to understand how money worked. I realised that you had to DO something to get money and once you had it you needed to take care of it and spend it wisely.

I had lots of jobs as a teenager. I worked in a chemist, washed pots in a restaurant, handed out change in an amusement arcade . . . you name it, I gave it a go. I loved working and I loved that I had my own money and could choose what I wanted to do with it. I was lucky that my 'needs' (*see page 63*) were taken care of by my parents, but I started to wonder what would happen when I had to pay for everything myself.

Thinking about life ahead is exciting and can be a little scary. I always knew I wanted my own business, but I had no idea what that would be. Trying to decide what you want to do and how you will earn your money can be confusing and it is natural to be a little anxious.

However, with the right knowledge and support you can have a happy and healthy relationship with money, which means that not only can you look after yourself and your family, you can have lots of fun too!

I'll be talking about earning money, spending money, borrowing money, business and much more!

ARE YOU READY TO TALK MONEY?

IT'S HARD TO IMAGINE WHAT LIFE WOULD
BE LIKE WITHOUT MONEY BECAUSE WE
USE IT EVERY DAY TO BUY THE THINGS
WE NEED AND WANT! MONEY GIVES
US SECURITY AND CHOICES.

# CHAPTER 1

# MONEY MAKES THE WORLD GO ROUND

## WHAT IS MONEY?

Money is what people use to buy things.
It is anything that is accepted as payment.
Today, we have two types of money – **cash**
(coins and banknotes) and **electronic money**
(e.g. bank transfers and bank cards).

## HAS MONEY ALWAYS BEEN AROUND?

Before money, there was a swapping system
called **bartering**, which people used to trade
things. It didn't always work well, though, as
people would need to find someone who wanted
what they had, and swap it when they wanted
it – imagine how tricky it would have been if
no one wanted to swap your cow for bread!

## HAVE WE ALWAYS USED CASH?

Cash has been around for ages . . . but it hasn't
always looked like it does today. The first
coins appeared over 2,500 years ago and
the first banknotes around 1,400 years ago,
but before that, people used things such as
shells and beads instead.

TODAY, IT DOESN'T MATTER WHAT SHAPE, SIZE OR COLOUR MONEY IS. IT WORKS BECAUSE **PEOPLE BELIEVE IN ITS VALUE** AND TRUST THEY WILL BE ABLE TO SWAP IT FOR THE THINGS THEY WANT.

## WHY IS A £10 NOTE WORTH £10?

Each banknote costs the same money to make, so why is a £10 note worth £10 and a £5 note worth £5? Well, it's all down to trust – we trust that we can exchange it for things, to the value that is written on the note. This is the same for coins. The fancy name for this is **fiat money**.

### DID YOU KNOW?

Until 1931, paper money in the UK was connected to the equivalent value of gold – a system called the **gold standard** – to help people trust its value. Today, we use a system called fiat money (where the government decides and backs its value). Since 2013, there haven't been any countries who use the gold standard.

## HOW ARE COINS MADE?

In money factories – called mints. Coins are made by melting metals in a furnace to create long strips. Round discs, called blanks, are then punched out. These blanks are then cleaned and stamped into coins.

UP TO 10,000 BLANKS CAN BE PUNCHED OUT IN A MINUTE!

COINS HAVEN'T ALWAYS BEEN ROUND – SQUARE COINS WERE USED IN INDIA ABOUT 2,400 YEARS AGO.

## WHAT ARE COINS MADE FROM?

Coins used to be gold or silver, but today they are usually made from a mixture of metals (such as nickel and copper), called an **alloy**.

## HOW ARE BANKNOTES MADE?

They are made by specialist printers. Detailed patterns are printed onto polymer (a thin, flexible plastic). Until recently, they were printed on paper, but polymer is harder to forge and lasts longer than paper banknotes.

## ARE BANKNOTES ECO-FRIENDLY?

Polymer banknotes last at least two-and-a-half times longer than paper ones, so this makes them more environmentally friendly. They can also be recycled and made into things, such as plant pots. Old British paper notes were composted and spread onto farmers' fields.

THE BANK OF ENGLAND HAS BANKNOTES WORTH £100 MILLION EACH — I'M NOT SURPRISED THEY ARE CALLED TITANS!

THEY AREN'T IN CIRCULATION, THOUGH, SO DON'T 'BANK' ON GETTING HOLD OF ONE! THEY ARE KEPT IN THE BANK OF ENGLAND, AND PLAY A VITAL ROLE BACKING THE VALUE OF SCOTTISH AND NORTHERN IRISH BANKNOTES.

## IS IT EASY TO MAKE COPIES (COUNTERFEITS) OF COINS AND BANKNOTES?

No! Coins and banknotes have special security features. Grab a £1 coin, for example, and you'll see features that help make it trickier to counterfeit:

- A hologram-like image that changes from a **£** to a **1** when seen at different angles.

- Grooves on alternate sides.

- Twelve sides.

- Tiny lettering on the inside rim.

- Made from two metals.

- A secret hidden feature to make it even harder to copy in the future!

Cash needs to be difficult to copy so that we don't lose trust in it. And fake money can hurt the economy by causing businesses to lose money (which affects the cost of what we buy!).

**FEWER THAN 1 IN 30,000 BANKNOTES WERE COUNTERFEIT IN THE UK IN 2023.**

Making copies of coins or banknotes is illegal. Usually, counterfeit money is spotted quickly and removed from circulation.

# FAKE MONEY

Although making copies of cash is very tricky,
some criminals still try. Here are some
who have tried, and failed . . .

Three men in the UK were jailed in 2020 and
2021 after police found counterfeit money
with a face value of £5.25 million!

In 2012, a man in Canada was caught with
$250 million (£194 million) in forged US banknotes.
It cost him around 325,000 Canadian dollars
(£189,000) to make them and he went to prison.
Now he has a consultancy company that helps
companies avoid getting their products faked!

IF YOU EVER SPOT
COUNTERFEIT CASH, HAND IT
TO THE POLICE – YOU WON'T GET
ANY MONEY AS IT IS WORTHLESS,
BUT IT WILL HELP POLICE
INVESTIGATIONS.

## WHY CAN'T WE JUST PRINT EXTRA MONEY?

Wouldn't that be brilliant? We could all have as much as we wanted! Sadly, it doesn't work like that. If we print more money, people can buy more stuff. If companies don't have more stuff to sell, they just put prices up, so you get less for your money. This is called **inflation**.

## IS INFLATION BAD?

Inflation is the increase in prices of things and means that over time you get fewer things for your money. So, today, a toy might cost £10, but in a few years' time, the same toy may cost £12. A small amount of inflation can be good as it means the economy is growing, but if it increases too quickly (**hyperinflation**) then that can be bad.

THE OPPOSITE OF INFLATION CAN HAPPEN WHEN PRICES FALL. SOUNDS GREAT, DOESN'T IT? NOT ALWAYS! IF YOU HAVE BORROWED MONEY AND WAGES GO DOWN, YOU HAVE LESS MONEY TO PAY THE DEBT.

WHAT DO YOU THINK THE OPPOSITE OF INFLATION IS CALLED?

Answer: Deflation.

## WHAT IS HYPERINFLATION?

This is when inflation increases very quickly, and it means that money is worth less and less. If a large amount of money is needed to buy anything, then people may stop trusting the system (and go back to bartering!). Don't worry, though – this is very, very rare, because governments do lots of things to keep inflation under control, such as increasing interest rates (see 'DID YOU KNOW?' below).

In 2008, Zimbabwe suffered hyperinflation because the government kept printing more money. Prices doubled every day and by July, inflation had reached 250,000,000%, which meant a sweet that previously cost one Zimbabwean dollar (Z$1), cost Z$250 million!

### DID YOU KNOW?

When inflation gets too high, the Bank of England can step in and increase interest rates. This does two things: borrowing money becomes more expensive and saving money earns more interest. This means people spend less and save more. If less money is being spent, then demand for things comes down, which can bring inflation down too.

## LET'S TALK ABOUT SUPPLY AND DEMAND

This is a good time to talk about these because they will come up a lot! **Supply** is how much of something there is, and **demand** is how much people want it. Say there is one pizza restaurant in town, it's popular and they charge high prices that people pay because they want pizza. Then another pizza place opens. What do you think happens to prices? Yep, prices get more competitive, which usually means prices go down or you get more for your money as each one tries to win your business.

### CHALLENGE

We have '50' tomatoes and '50' people. Do prices go up, down or stay the same when . . .

- 1. Fifty people want one tomato each?
- 2. Fifty people want two tomatoes each?
- 3. Half the people want one tomato each?

Answers:
- 1. Prices stay the same.
- 2. Prices go up.
- 3. Prices go down.

# THINGS THAT AFFECT DEMAND

**SEASONS**
For example, in winter there's less demand for ice cream and more for woolly hats.

**INCOME**
When people's income increases, they can afford to buy more so demand goes up. And demand goes down when income decreases.

**TRENDS**
Demand can go up if something becomes 'in fashion', such as the latest book or food. It can also go down if it becomes 'out of fashion'.

**CHOICE**
If there are lots of different types of something, then demand can go down, or go up if it is rare.

**PRICE**
Usually, demand goes down when the price of something goes up.

**EXPECTATION**
Demand can increase if people think the price of something is about to go up.

## SHOULD WE ALL HAVE THE SAME AMOUNT OF MONEY?

It would be nice, wouldn't it? But even if we all started with the same amount of money, our different choices would change things pretty quickly. We might choose to work long hours and save money or work fewer hours and spend money. Our choices can affect the amount of money we each have . . . and we have lots of choices!

**THE BANK OF ENGLAND'S INFLATION CALCULATOR SHOWS THAT THIRTY YEARS AGO YOU COULD BUY TWICE AS MUCH WITH £1 COMPARED TO TODAY!**

## PEOPLE SAY £1 IS NOT WORTH £1 ANY MORE. WHAT DO THEY MEAN?

£1 is still worth £1, but what really matters is what, and how much, you can buy with it . . . and who decides that? It's down to inflation (*see page 16*). So, what people really mean is, you can't buy as much as you used to with your £1!

## DO WE STILL NEED CASH?

Good question! More people are using digital money, so why bother with cash? Well, with cash it is easy to see how much you are spending and not spend more than you have, it is safe from online thieves, spending is private (with digital money, data is gathered on you – *see page 79*), and many older and vulnerable people don't use digital money.

**WE MAY USE LESS CASH NOW, BUT THERE'S A LONG WAY TO GO UNTIL WE GO COMPLETELY CASHLESS.**

## ARE 1P AND 2P COINS POINTLESS?

When 1p and 2p coins were introduced in 1971, a loaf of bread cost 9p. We needed small coins to pay the right money or get the right change, but do we still need them? Well, they still have their uses. For a start, they can help us save – pop spare coins in a jar and you'll soon have something worthwhile! Getting rid of small coins would also cause inflation as prices would get rounded up, e.g. 99p would become £1 (a 1% price increase)!

IN 1984, THE HALFPENNY COIN WAS REMOVED FROM CIRCULATION IN THE UK.

THE BRITISH POUND IS THE WORLD'S
OLDEST CURRENCY THAT IS STILL
IN USE TODAY. IT DATES BACK
ABOUT 1,200 YEARS.

## WHY CAN'T I USE BRITISH POUNDS IN OTHER COUNTRIES?

British pounds are the units of money the UK
government says can be used in this country,
but each country or area has their own unit.
This is called **currency**. Because each country
is different, their unit of currency will have
a different value to a £1. When we go abroad,
we need to exchange pounds for a different
currency, such as yen in Japan or rupee in India.

## DOES EVERY COUNTRY HAVE ITS OWN CURRENCY?

Most do, but sometimes a group of countries will
agree to have the same currency to make buying
and selling from each other easier. Often they are
close by or have some common history, or they do
a lot of business with each other. An example of
this are the countries in Europe that have joined
the EU and use the euro as currency.

## WHAT IS AN EXCHANGE RATE?

It's how much one currency is worth against another. For example, how many dollars you can exchange for a pound.

## WHO DECIDES THE EXCHANGE RATE?

It's all down to supply and demand (*see page 18*). Exchange rates go up and down according to how popular the currency is, and that depends on what is happening in a country (e.g. whether there is a stable government, a natural disaster or war).

### CHALLENGE

The Bank of Deborah is giving exchange rates below for British pounds (GBP), e.g. one pound would get you 1.15 euros. For each currency, work out how much you would receive in exchange for £10.

US dollar (USD): 1.22
euro (EUR): 1.15
Japanese yen (JPY): 181.74
Chinese yuan (CNY): 8.90
Australian dollar (AUD): 1.91

Answers: 12.2 US dollars, 11.5 euros, 1,817 Japanese yen, 89 Chinese yuan, 19.1 Australian dollars.

## WHAT IS 'INVISIBLE' MONEY?

When you buy something with a credit card, or online, you are using digital money. It's invisible because it only exists electronically – you can't see it or touch it. You are probably using it already if you buy things with a card, smartphone or app.

~~~~~~

THE FIRST ELECTRIC MONEY TRANSFERS
WERE LAUNCHED BY WESTERN UNION
IN THE US AS EARLY AS 1871.

~~~~~~

## WHAT ARE CRYPTOCURRENCIES?

An **asset** is something you own and you can sell for money. **Cryptocurrencies**, or crypto, are a digital asset. They are a kind of digital money; except they are issued by companies or private individuals – people like you and me! Instead of money records being held at a central place, such as a bank, they are shared across a network of computers, or 'nodes'. These are protected by codes to make sure crypto can be created and exchanged only by the people who use them.

CRYPTOCURRENCY TRANSACTIONS
USE DATA INSTEAD OF CASH.

## HOW DOES CRYPTO WORK?

Cryptocurrencies use cryptography (writing and deciphering codes) to check, issue and record each transaction or exchange. Each transaction is represented by something called a **block**, which is timestamped, added to the last block in the chain and shared across the network. This is called **blockchain technology**. The timestamp can't be changed, so it is hard to fake or steal . . . making it very safe, though not completely safe!

## WHAT IS BITCOIN?

Bitcoin (BTC) was the first successful cryptocurrency (launched in 2009), but there are loads now, such as ethereum (ETH) and tether (USDT). The people who started bitcoin decided there would only ever be 21 million bitcoins, so the more people that have them, the harder they are to find or 'mine' (*see page 28*). And the rarer they become, the more valuable they are!

THE FIRST THING BOUGHT WITH BITCOIN WAS PIZZA! IN 2010, LASZLO HANYECZ BOUGHT TWO PIZZAS FOR 10,000 BITCOINS (WORTH AROUND US$25 AT THE TIME).

## WHY ARE CRYPTOCURRENCIES WORTH ANYTHING?

Because we believe they are – same as pounds! If enough people believe in their value and buy them, the price goes up. If everyone sees the price going up, they want to buy them too. However, there aren't enough for everyone, so guess what . . . the price goes up again (supply and demand!). BUT say something happens to make buyers nervous and they stop believing, prices can tumble fast. This makes crypto a very risky investment.

## WHAT ARE THE RISKS OF CRYPTOCURRENCIES?

They aren't backed by banks or governments, so it's hard to get help if something goes wrong. And you need to watch out for theft by hackers and scams – criminals can trick or lure people into helping them by offering payment if they transfer stolen money through their bank account. People who move this stolen money are called **money mules**.

IN 2017, THE PRICE OF ONE BITCOIN PEAKED AT ABOUT £15,400, BUT IN 2019, ONE WAS WORTH JUST £5,400. BY 2021, THE PRICE OF ONE REACHED £50,000! I WONDER WHAT IT WILL BE WORTH IN THE FUTURE!

## MONEY MULES

**Money laundering** is when money from fraudulent and illegal activities is moved and processed to make it look legitimate or 'clean'. Using money mules is becoming a common way of doing this. If someone asks if you can move their money in and out of your bank account or crypto wallet for payment, be highly suspicious and ask yourself 'Why?'. You might unwittingly be agreeing to become a money mule, which is criminal.

MONEY MULES CAN ALSO BE CALLED SMURFS.

## SCAMS TO WATCH OUT FOR INCLUDE . . .

- You get a random email from a web-based email service or social media contact promising extra cash for little or no effort.

- You are asked to open a bank account, trading account or crypto wallet to receive money, and are then asked to transfer that money to another account, keeping some for yourself.

27

## HOW DO YOU GET CRYPTOCURRENCY?

You can buy it online, or if you have access to super powerful computers, you can 'mine' them. Crypto miners don't need a shovel and a hard hat! These miners solve difficult mathematical equations to verify and add transactions to the blockchain network and are rewarded for their work with crypto.

## WHAT IS A BITCOIN FARM?

It takes special hardware, software and LOTS of electricity to mine bitcoin, so people join 'pools' (groups of people doing the same thing so they can share the costs). The biggest pools are called bitcoin (or crypto) mining farms.

## SHOULD I BUY CRYPTOCURRENCY?

You may be too young – many have age limits because of the risks. Their values jump up and down quickly, so before handing over money, learn about how they work, understand the risks (*see page 26*), and keep an eye on the things that might make them more or less valuable, such as global financial events.

## CAN I BUY THINGS WITH CRYPTOCURRENCY?

It used to be hard, but it is getting easier as people trust them more. Different cryptocurrencies have different values, though, and some will charge you more than others when you buy something or move money, so always check before you buy.

## IS BITCOIN BETTER FOR THE ENVIRONMENT?

Because bitcoins are digital, you'd think they are better for the environment, but no! An incredible amount of power is needed for the countless computers being used in the race to mine bitcoins.

IT IS ESTIMATED THAT 'MINING' ONE BITCOIN HAS THE SAME CARBON FOOTPRINT AS USING A CREDIT CARD 330,000 TIMES!

## ARE OTHER CRYPTOCURRENCIES ECO-FRIENDLY?

Some cryptocurrencies, such as ethereum, have recently come up with a way to reduce their carbon emissions through a software upgrade called 'proof of stake'.

WHAT ARE THE TOP THREE
THINGS THAT MAKE YOU
HAPPY, BUT DON'T
COST ANYTHING?

## WILL MONEY MAKE ME HAPPY?

Some of my happiest moments have been laughing with friends, spending time with loved ones, throwing balls for the dogs to catch . . . with not a credit card in sight!

Life is easier when you don't have to worry about how you will pay for important things like food and bills, though, and having savings can help you feel more safe and secure. Plus, we all need some fun! So having money for treats, such as concert tickets, can feel good, too.

SPENDING MONEY ON
OTHER PEOPLE OR GIVING
MONEY TO CHARITY CAN
MAKE PEOPLE FEEL HAPPIER.

# CHAPTER 2

## EARNING MONEY

## HOW CAN I GET MONEY?

It's great to be given money as a gift or to be paid an allowance. However, if you want more money, you could sell things you don't need any more or do things that family, friends or neighbours will pay you for, like cleaning cars or babysitting, or look for a job with the help of an adult.

IF YOU'RE 13 OR OVER, SPEAK TO YOUR PARENTS/GUARDIANS ABOUT GETTING A REGULAR PART-TIME JOB TO EARN MONEY. EARNING YOUR OWN MONEY FEELS GOOD AND CAN BE FUN TOO!

AT 13, YOU CAN WORK FOR UP TO 12 HOURS A WEEK DURING TERM TIME OR 25 HOURS A WEEK DURING THE HOLIDAYS. THE OLDER YOU ARE, THE MORE HOURS YOU CAN WORK!

## WHAT PART-TIME JOB COULD YOU DO?
## HERE IS SOME INSPIRATION . . .

- Delivering newspapers
- Walking dogs/Pet-sitting
- Cutting grass/Weeding
- Working in a shop
- Being a tour guide
- Inputting data

HARRY STYLES'
FIRST JOB WAS
IN A BAKERY.

FIRST JOBS CAN BE DAUNTING, BUT AS WELL
AS EARNING YOU MONEY, THEY GIVE YOU
A CHANCE TO MEET NEW PEOPLE, LEARN
HOW TO WORK WITH OTHERS AND HELP
YOU THINK ABOUT YOUR FUTURE CAREER.

TAYLOR SWIFT'S FIRST
JOB WAS PICKING PRAYING
MANTIS PODS OFF CHRISTMAS TREES
SO THEY WOULDN'T HATCH IN
CUSTOMERS' HOUSES.

## WHERE CAN I FIND MY FIRST JOB?

How about starting by looking where you live? Are there any shops, restaurants or other businesses with jobs that might suit you? Pop in to speak to a manager or send your CV to places where you'd like to work or do some work experience. You never know, they might have something for you. Ask friends and family for suggestions or to help you look for a part-time job online.

YOU DON'T HAVE TO FIND THE PERFECT FIRST JOB OR STAY IN THE SAME JOB OR CAREER FOR EVER.

NEVER GIVE UP. IF YOU REALLY WANT SOMETHING, DON'T BE DISHEARTENED IF YOU GET LOTS OF 'NOES'. IT HAPPENS TO ALL OF US!

## WHAT IS A CV AND WHY DO I NEED ONE?

Your CV tells a potential employer all about you, your experience and why you would be perfect for the job. It's your first contact with them, so try to make a great first impression.

CV IS SHORT FOR *CURRICULUM VITAE* IN LATIN, WHICH TRANSLATES TO 'THE COURSE OF LIFE'.

## WHAT DO I PUT IN A COVER LETTER?

A cover letter is sent with your CV. It's usually about three to five paragraphs long and is a way to introduce yourself, say who you are and why you are sending your CV. Tell them which job you are interested in, where you saw it and why you think you are the perfect fit. If you are sending a CV to see if a company has any jobs available, tell them what you might be interested in and why you would be excited to work for them.

## BE YOUR OWN BOSS

If you don't want to work for a company, you could
think about starting your own company. The best
news is you don't need millions of pounds to do it.
All I needed for my first business was flowers,
a small table and a handwritten sign!
What could you do? Perhaps . . . design T-shirts?
Sell greetings cards?

A BOY IN THE US STARTED HIS
OWN YOUTUBE CHANNEL WHEN HE WAS
YOUNG. HE NOW EARNS OVER
A MILLION DOLLARS A YEAR!

A TEEN FROM LONDON, UK, STARTED
HIS OWN DIGITAL PUBLISHING COMPANY
WHEN HE WAS JUST 11.

AN ECO-COSMETICS BUSINESS WAS
SET UP BY A YOUNG GIRL IN THE
UK AFTER WINNING A SCHOOL
COMPETITION. SIX YEARS LATER, IT WAS
GENERATING OVER £100,000 A YEAR.

*See Chapter 6* for tips on starting a business.

## SHOULD I VOLUNTEER?

Money is not the only reward for work. Volunteering to help others or to support projects you care about is a great way to gain important skills and experience to add to your CV, and to meet new people and make new friends. **IS THERE ANY VOLUNTEER WORK THAT YOU COULD DO?**

IT'S EASIER TO VOLUNTEER AND DONATE MONEY IF YOU HAVE TIME AND MONEY, SO DON'T WORRY IF YOU AREN'T ABLE TO VOLUNTEER OR DONATE YET.

## HOW DO I RAISE MONEY FOR CHARITY?

If you've ever seen someone running a marathon dressed as a giant banana, the chances are they were raising money for charity. Start by setting yourself a target of how much you want to raise, then think about what you can do. Perhaps you could take part in a sponsored walk or set up a talent show and ask for donations? There are other ways to raise money too. Perhaps you could do chores, sell things you don't need, sell cakes . . .

FUNDRAISING CAN BE CHALLENGING,
BUT IT CAN ALSO BE FUN
AND REWARDING.

# INTERVIEW WITH
# SOPHIE ELLIS-BEXTOR

Singer-songwriter

## WHAT LED YOU TO THE JOB YOU HAVE NOW?

I started singing in a band at 16, and ideas about becoming a ballerina, a nurse or a journalist fell away. I literally didn't have a second thought about any other job after that. I finished my A-levels at 18 and went straight off on tour around the UK with my band. And I've been singing ever since!

## HOW IMPORTANT IS MONEY TO YOU?

Money gives you choice, and choice gives you more power and autonomy. So, I think money is pretty important, but it is definitely not my motivating factor. You've got to try and find a way to keep a roof over your head and happiness in your heart.

## WHY DO YOU GIVE MONEY TO CHARITY?

I'm a very fortunate person and I have a lot of lovely things in my life, so being able to lend my time – to sing, to do what I can to support charities – is the least I can do. I should do more, really.

## ARE YOU A SPENDER OR A SAVER?

Somewhere in the middle. I've always liked giving myself presents, but luckily for me my taste is pretty cheap – I'm happy with a second-hand dress. But, that being said, I've had moments in my life when money has run very, very thin, so it has been important to save and be more prudent.

## WHAT MONEY ADVICE WOULD YOU GIVE TO YOUR TEENAGE SELF?

You've got to understand what lifestyle you're hoping to achieve, what it will take to keep that consistent, and then manage it. And if you want what you can't afford, you've got to go back to the drawing board. I think it's about living within your means and doing what you can to budget, so that your monthly outgoings, the way you live your life and your spending, are at a realistic level you can sustain. And if you come into different periods of your life, where things are going better or worse, then you can adjust accordingly, but I think your day-to-day spending has got to be realistic.

## WHAT'S YOUR FAVOURITE THING TO DO THAT DOESN'T COST MUCH MONEY?

I love walking – it's so good for my head. And I also love playing with my kids, drawing and dancing!

## WHAT'S A PAYSLIP?

When you get a regular job, your employer will give you a **payslip** (either electronic or paper) as a record of how much you have earned and over what period. There are usually lots of other numbers and info on it too, *see page 41* for a heads-up on what it all means.

KEEP PAYSLIPS FOR AT LEAST 22 MONTHS AFTER EACH TAX YEAR ENDS, JUST IN CASE THERE'S A MISTAKE WITH WHAT YOU'VE BEEN PAID.

YOU'LL NEED YOUR PAYSLIPS WHEN YOU WANT TO BUY OR RENT SOMEWHERE TO LIVE TO PROVE HOW MUCH YOU EARN.

## TAX CODE
A CODE ISSUED BY HMRC (HIS MAJESTY'S REVENUE AND CUSTOMS) TELLING YOUR EMPLOYER HOW MUCH TAX TO DEDUCT.

## NATIONAL INSURANCE
HOW MUCH WILL GO TO THE GOVERNMENT IF YOU ARE 16 OR OVER, TO HELP PAY FOR THINGS SUCH AS STATE PENSIONS.

## PENSION CONTRIBUTION
HOW MUCH WILL GO TOWARDS YOUR PERSONAL PENSION.

## STUDENT LOANS
HOW MUCH WILL GO TOWARDS PAYING BACK A STUDENT LOAN, IF YOU HAVE ONE.

## PAYROLL NUMBER
A UNIQUE NUMBER — TO MAKE SURE YOUR MONEY GOES TO YOU!

**Mr Joe Bloggs**
16 Apple Street, Tree Town, AP1 2PZ

| 123456 | | | |
|---|---|---|---|
| **Earnings** | **Amount** | **Deductions** | **Amount** |
| Gross pay | £xxx | Tax (code 123B) | £xxx |
| Net pay | £xxx | NI | £xxx |
| Tax | £xxx | Pension | £xxx |
| | | Student Loan | £xxx |
| **Allowances** | | **Amount Paid** | **£xxx** |
| xxx | £xxx | | |

## GROSS PAY
HOW MUCH YOU HAVE EARNED IN TOTAL — BEFORE ANY DEDUCTIONS E.G. INCOME TAX. (SEE PAGE 48).

## NET PAY
HOW MUCH MONEY YOU WILL ACTUALLY RECEIVE — AFTER ANY DEDUCTIONS E.G. INCOME TAX (SEE PAGE 48).

## INCOME TAX
HOW MUCH WILL GO TO THE GOVERNMENT, IF YOU EARN OVER A CERTAIN AMOUNT. (SEE PAGE 48).

## ALLOWANCES
ANY INCOME THAT YOU WOULD NORMALLY PAY TAX ON BUT YOU DON'T HAVE TO.

## AMOUNT PAID
NET PAY MINUS ANY DEDUCTIONS.

## WHAT CAREER SHOULD I CHOOSE?

Teacher, plumber, accountant, games developer, chef, forensic scientist . . . with so many possible jobs, it can seem overwhelming, but start by thinking about what is more important to you – doing a career you love and could be happy doing until you retire or earning enough cash for the lifestyle you want? It could be both!

I ALWAYS KNEW I WANTED TO HAVE MY OWN BUSINESS AND WOULD NEED TO UNDERSTAND NUMBERS. I WASN'T GOOD AT MATHS (I KNOW THAT SOUNDS ODD!), BUT I LOVE THE WAY NUMBERS PAINT A PICTURE – THEY ARE LIKE A MAP TO ME. I CAN EASILY SEE WHERE SOMETHING IS GOING RIGHT OR WRONG!

## WHAT IF I CAN'T DECIDE WHAT CAREER TO DO?

Don't panic – you're not alone! Try talking to different people about their jobs or look for some work experience. You won't have all the answers, but it's the thinking and exploring that counts.

## WHAT'S AN APPRENTICESHIP?

It's a paid job that also offers practical training in a chosen career, as well as classroom learning.

## SHOULD I DO AN APPRENTICESHIP?

First-hand experience is a great way to learn, and there are loads of apprenticeships you can choose. Once you know what you want to do, you can decide if the best way to reach your goal is by going to college or university, or joining a company as an apprentice.

> IF YOU WANT TO DO SOMETHING BUT YOU'RE SCARED, IF IT DOESN'T HARM OTHERS OR YOURSELF, JUST DO IT.

JOE LYCETT, COMEDIAN

# INTERVIEW WITH
# JOE LYCETT

Comedian

## WHAT WAS YOUR FIRST JOB?

In a call centre selling soffits and guttering.
It was a grim experience because I didn't know
what soffits were and, to be honest, I still don't.
I left after a few weeks and never looked back.

## WHAT LED YOU TO DO THE JOB YOU HAVE NOW?

I am someone who likes to try lots of different
things. I see life as like a big table of tapas – you
have a little bit of this, experience some of that.
At university I tried doing graphic design, art,
making films, being an actor. I also tried stand-up
comedy, and that was the bit of tapas that I got
the most enjoyment out of (like halloumi). I still
did the other things, but a bit less, and once
comedy started paying properly, they became
less like tapas and more like a side salad.

## WHAT IS YOUR FAVOURITE THING TO DO
## THAT DOESN'T INVOLVE MONEY?

Tap dancing at 3am.

## HOW IMPORTANT IS MONEY TO YOU?

Money is undoubtedly important, but it's not everything. I am very lucky that I earn well, but I earn less than I probably could. I am careful with what I say yes to: if I'm not going to enjoy it, then people around me won't enjoy it, and all I'll have to show are some numbers on a screen. I appreciate this a privileged position to be in, but whenever I hear someone saying they don't like their job, I always try and convince them to change it!

## ARE YOU A SPENDER OR A SAVER?

Both. I learned the hard way that a freelancer has to save money for their tax. I developed a rule with everything I earn: the minute it hits my account, I split it in half. One half goes into a savings account, the other stays in my current account. Tax will never be half, however much you earn. It will always be less, so at the end of the year there's a little bonus money left over.

Once I've saved money for my tax and bills, I usually spend money on good food, the occasional gadget and sometimes art (which I see as an investment that also happens to look nice).

## WHY DON'T ALL JOBS PAY THE SAME?

If you have studied and trained for years to get certain skills, should you be rewarded with a bigger salary? Is it fair that junior doctors earn less per hour than some baristas? Some industries, like finance and technology, make more money than others, so they can pay their employees more. Supply and demand also play a part. If there is a high demand for certain skills, but not many people have them, employers need to pay more to compete with other companies. But what do you think – should all jobs be paid the same?

## WHAT DOES MINIMUM WAGE MEAN?

It's the lowest amount of money you can be paid each hour you work by law when you are over school leaving age, which usually means 16. It is set by the government to help people meet their basic needs. If you are under 21, it is called **minimum wage**, and if you are 21 or older, it is called **living wage** (but really it's the same thing!).

### CHALLENGE
Minimum wage depends on age – see if you can find out what it would be between 16–18, 18–20 and 21 and over.

## WHAT ARE THE PROS AND CONS OF MINIMUM WAGE?

Minimum wage can be a good thing because it means fairer pay and less poverty, BUT it can also mean that low-skilled jobs are cut when business isn't good, so getting it right is a balancing act for the government.

## WHAT DOES REAL LIVING WAGE MEAN?

The Living Wage Foundation is a campaigning organisation that looks at the cost of a real basket of shopping, and other goods and services the average household spends money on, and works out how much you need to earn to cover it. This is called the real living wage. This isn't law, but some companies use it as a minimum because it takes into account the real cost of living.

## WHAT IS A ZERO-HOURS CONTRACT?

A **zero-hours contract** means there are no guarantees on how many hours you will be offered, or even if you will be offered any hours at all! It works the other way too – if you are offered hours, you don't have to work them. This might be good for your employer as they only pay you when they need you, but it can be tough for you to plan and budget.

ONE OF THE FIRST KNOWN TAXES IN THE UK WAS CALLED DANEGELD. ANGLO-SAXON LANDOWNERS PAID IT TO RAISE MONEY FOR PROTECTION AGAINST VIKING INVADERS.

## WHAT TYPES OF TAXES ARE THERE IN THE UK?

There are three main taxes in the UK, which are . . .

- **Income Tax:** Money collected from earnings that are over a certain threshold (decided by the government). It's collected by your employer and paid to HMRC, the government department responsible for tax.

- **National Insurance:** Money collected by your employer and used for certain benefits, such as the State Pension.

- **VAT (Value Added Tax):** This is known as a sales tax – it is paid on most things you buy (some things, such as books, are exempt). The place you are buying from collects the tax from you when you buy an item and passes it to the government.

But there are more! Have you heard of these ones?

- **Capital Gains Tax:** If you sell certain assets – such as shares in a business or a second home – at a higher price than you paid for them, this is called capital gains, and tax is paid on the profit. (You get a certain amount of tax-free allowance.)

- **Inheritance Tax:** When someone dies, the value of everything they own (houses, cash, investments, cars, life insurance . . .) is added together. Then everything they owe (debt) is deducted. If the amount left is more than the threshold (currently £325,000), tax must be paid on the amount above the threshold.

- **Corporation Tax:** A tax on the profit of a corporation or company.

### DID YOU KNOW?

Governments can change the amounts of tax we pay and introduce new ones. There have been some interesting ones throughout history! There have been taxes on fireplaces, glass, dice, clocks, tea, wallpaper, candles, soap, and there was even a tax on buying playing cards until 1960.

## WHY CAN'T WE KEEP ALL THE MONEY WE EARN?

If you earn over a certain amount of money in any one year (the **threshold**), you will pay income tax. Sound unfair? Not really . . . because the government needs money to pay for the things we all use.

WHEN YOU START WORK, ASK HMRC QUESTIONS ABOUT YOUR TAX CODE TO MAKE SURE YOU ARE PAYING THE RIGHT AMOUNT OF TAX. MANY PEOPLE START ON AN EMERGENCY RATE, WHICH IS HIGHER THAN IT SHOULD BE!

## WHERE DOES TAX GO?

The government spends it on the things we all need and benefit from, such as education, health and security. Taxes also go towards helping the economy: for example, through supporting businesses and foreign trade, and funding things like the arts and protecting the environment.

## DOES EVERYONE PAY THE SAME AMOUNT OF TAX?

In the UK we have something called a **progressive tax system**. It means that the more you earn, the higher the portion of your earnings you pay in tax. This is because the more money you have, the more you are able to pay, and it is meant to make things more equal.

## HOW DO I PAY MY TAX?

If you start working for a company, you won't need to worry about working out if you should pay tax or how much. That is your employer's job. You will be given a **tax code** by the government that tells your employer how much income tax to deduct and pass to HMRC.

## DO I PAY TAX IF I WORK FOR MYSELF (SELF EMPLOYED)?

Yes, but it's down to you! You must tell HMRC that you are responsible for working out your tax. This is called **self assessment**. To help work out how much tax to pay, you fill in something called a tax return. It will ask lots of questions about how much money you have earned and what money you have spent to earn it (e.g. on outgoings), so you need to keep good records!

## WHAT IF THE GOVERNMENT NEEDS MORE MONEY?

Just like us, they can borrow it. They don't ask a bank for a loan like we do, though. Instead, the government sells **bonds**. Bonds are basically a loan to the government for a set time on a fixed rate of interest. They are mainly bought by large banks, pension funds and insurance companies, but some bonds are offered to members of the public – such as premium bonds.

### DID YOU KNOW?

If you own **premium bonds**, then you are lending the government your money. Instead of paying you to use it, the government gives you the chance to win some more every month. The more bonds you have, the higher chance you have of winning. Sometimes these are called 'lottery bonds'.

## HOW CAN GOVERNMENTS PAY FOR EMERGENCIES?

They can borrow from the International Monetary Fund (IMF), but this is really only for temporary emergencies. The amount a government borrows in total is called the **National Debt**. Some countries have huge debts worth trillions of US dollars.

THE TOTAL AMOUNT THE UK GOVERNMENT OWES IS ABOUT £2.5 TRILLION!

A TRILLION IS ONE MILLION MILLION (1,000,000,000,000). THAT'S A LOT OF ZEROES!

## WHAT IS AN ECONOMY?

On the most basic level, it's the way people make and spend their money. An economy can be big or small: your local village, town, city, region, country or even the world! Money is constantly moving around, so when you're talking about an economy, you're looking at how much money is moving, where it is going and what's causing it to move.

## WHO IS IN CHARGE OF THE UK ECONOMY?

The government. Different departments manage different things. For example, the treasury's job is to decide how the government raises money and where it is spent, and comes up with a plan to help the economy stay healthy. The Office for National Statistics (ONS) gathers and analyses economic information to help the government with its decision making.

## WHY DOES THE ECONOMY MATTER TO ME?

When the economy is growing, we feel better off, there are lots of jobs, plenty of goods to buy and sell, and great public services because lots of people are paying tax for the government to spend on them. If it isn't doing well, then there is less demand for goods and services, so businesses might shut down and people can lose their jobs.

## HOW DO WE MEASURE THE ECONOMY?

First, we need to know what the UK's **Gross Domestic Product** is – GDP to you and me! This is how we work it out for each quarter (three months):

ALL THE MONEY SPENT IN THE UK + NET EXPORTS = GDP

THE VALUE OF THE STUFF SOLD ABROAD MINUS THE VALUE OF STUFF BOUGHT FROM ABROAD.

BUT to see if the economy is REALLY growing (because we are making and selling more and it's not just growing because prices are going up – inflation), we need to take off the inflation to work out the REAL GDP.

When we know our real GDP for that quarter, we check if it's gone up or down on the last one. UP = Good; DOWN = Bad. If real GDP falls and is still falling by the third quarter, we have gone into a recession . . .

## IS GDP IS MISLEADING?

Yes! Bigger countries with more people often have a higher GDP, but to know what that really means for the people who live there, you need to know something called **GDP per capita** (per person). To work this out, you take the total GDP and divide it by the number of people in that country (its population). But, even then there are problems! We know that not everyone has the same amount of money, so the per capita number doesn't really reflect the reality. It also doesn't take the 'cost of living' into account. A high GDP with a very high cost of living would mean the people living in a country could be worse off than someone in a lower GDP country with a lower cost of living.

Some people argue that GDP should also measure the health and the well-being of a country. After all, that is what really matters!

# CHAPTER 3

## SAVING MONEY

# QUIZ: ARE YOU A SPENDER, A SAVER OR AN ENTREPRENEUR?

For each scenario, pick the answer
that is closest to what you would do.

**1. You find a £10 note in your pocket. Do you ...**

a) Go out and buy a treat for yourself?

b) Pay it into your bank account?

c) Go out and buy some snacks to sell
at a profit to your friends?

**2. When you get birthday/Christmas money,
or your allowance, do you ...**

a) Go out to your favourite café with your friends.
Time for a huge hot chocolate?

b) Start making your budget spreadsheet: thinking
about what things you have coming up that you
need to buy, and how much you have left over?

c) Use it to buy materials for your brand-new idea
(e.g. making jewellery to sell)?

### 3. You need a new bag. Would you . . .

a) Buy one quickly from the nearest shop?

b) Look at different shops in person and online to compare prices?

c) Try to make your own (and think maybe others might like to buy one, too)?

### 4. You accidentally break an object. What do you do?

a) Ask your family for money to buy a new one.

b) Think about whether you need a new one and if you do, shop around to see what to spend your money on.

c) Try to fix it.

### 5. You are planning to open a bank account. What do you look for when doing your research?

a) A bank account is a bank account, right? The main thing is to pick one and start using it.

b) A savings account with a good interest rate.

c) A branch close to where you live, so you can pay in and withdraw money easily.

*Turn over to see whether you're a spender, a saver or an entrepreneur . . .*

*If you answered . . .*

### MOSTLY AS = SPENDER

You like to live in the moment, rather than focussing on the future. Is there something you would really like, but can't quite afford? Put a bit of money aside each week to save up for it.

### MOSTLY BS = SAVER

You are a forward-thinker who loves planning and the thrill of a good deal. But don't let your saving goals stop you having fun sometimes.

### MOSTLY CS = ENTREPRENEUR

You are a saver, but are happy to spend money if it feeds into your business ideas, and will possibly make you more money. Put in time for planning and research to help your ideas take off.

BEAR IN MIND, TO BE A SPENDER, YOU DO HAVE TO BE A BIT OF A SAVER – SPENDING MONEY YOU DON'T HAVE MEANS YOU WILL GET INTO DEBT!

## WHAT IS A BUDGET?

A **budget** is a fancy word for a money plan over a certain amount of time. It compares how much money you have coming **IN** (e.g. from an allowance or wages), how much is going **OUT** (such as buying tickets or paying a bill) and **WHEN** this happens. It also looks at the bigger picture, so you can save money for larger things or on things you know might be needed in the future.

- Calculate your money coming in and your money going out. If more is going out than coming in, you'll need to cut back on your spending.

- If your money going out is less than your money coming in, you can save or invest the money.

- Keep some 'emergency funds' for unexpected costs and regularly review your budget.

> I REVIEW MY SPENDING EVERY MONTH AGAINST MONEY I HAVE COMING IN AND HOW MUCH I'D LIKE TO SAVE. I CAN THEN MAKE BETTER DECISIONS ON HOW I NEED TO MANAGE MY MONEY.

ANDY JEFFERIES, CO-FOUNDER OF DOCK & BAY – QUICK-DRYING TOWELS.

## WHY DO I NEED TO BUDGET?

Actually, you want to budget because it's going to keep you in control of your money, and help you save and plan for things in the future. **BUDGETING IS A POWERFUL HABIT TO GET INTO.** Starting now, when your budget is simple, is great practice for when there are many things to juggle.

## WHAT ARE NEEDS AND WANTS?

**Needs** are the things you must have, like food, clothes and shelter. **Wants** are nice to have, but not necessary. **NEEDS SHOULD COME FIRST AND THEN YOU CAN LOOK AT WANTS.**

### LITTLE THINGS ADD UP

Are there things you buy regularly? Say, a chocolate bar? Work out how many you buy each month on average and how much that costs. It may not seem much each time, but over a year it can be a lot!

It's good to have treats sometimes, but think about whether there is an opportunity to save money. Perhaps buying less frequently? Or in a multi-pack? Or choosing a cheaper brand?

## HOW CAN I AFFORD SOMETHING EXPENSIVE?

Using your budget (*see page 62*), check if you have money left over after you've paid for necessities (your needs). If you do, well done! You have a choice to make . . . you can spend your money now or save it! Is there something you really want? Perhaps that is a bit pricey? Work out exactly how much it costs (including added costs like delivery or bills).

Then go back to your budget and work out how much you can save each week. How long will it take until you can afford to buy what you want? If you're patient, you'll get there – or if the wait is too long, you might choose to give up something else to save more or try to earn more and get it quicker!

AIM TO SAVE AROUND 20% OF YOUR MONEY, BECAUSE SAVING A LITTLE EACH WEEK IS EASIER THAN TRYING TO FIND A LOT OF MONEY VERY QUICKLY.

EVERY TIME YOU BUY YOURSELF SOMETHING NON–ESSENTIAL, ASK YOURSELF: DO I WANT THIS MORE THAN THE THING I AM SAVING FOR? IF THE ANSWER IS NO, DON'T BUY IT.

# RANA AND TOM

Rana and Tom are great friends but they are very different with their money.

Rana wants new trainers. She has £100 to buy them, but she finds some brand-new ones she likes online for £80. She then spends the remaining £20 on a top on sale from the same website.

Tom also wants new trainers but a different style and has £100 to buy them. He finds the ones he wants but they cost £95. He then decides to save the £5 he has left.

## WHO DO YOU THINK IS GOOD WITH THEIR MONEY?

Let's take Rana – if she was going to save up to buy the top anyway, buying it on sale with the money she had left over from her trainers is clever. BUT if she only bought it because she had £20 left, it may have been better to save the money for something she really wanted later.

What about Tom? Tom spent more on his trainers, but he got what he wanted and wasn't tempted to spend the £5 he had left. That could go towards something he REALLY wants in the future.

## HOW TO AFFORD SOMETHING EXPENSIVE

Say you want to buy a phone. First off, find out what the best deal is. **THE BEST DEAL IS NOT ALWAYS THE BEST PRICE!** It depends on what else they offer. You could use an online comparison site to help you, but let's try it for ourselves . . .

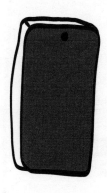

**STEP 1:** Find the phone you want to buy and work out how much you will have to pay immediately (**upfront costs**), and how much you will pay each month. Add all that up to find out the **total cost**. Explore deals from different providers.

**STEP 2:** Write down any **freebies** the different network providers are offering, and find out what they are worth. Ignore the stuff you don't want – there's no point getting something free that you won't use or already have!

**STEP 3:** Come up with a budget (money plan) that shows how and when you are going to get the money, and where you are going to save it. Then find someone you trust to talk to about your choices, your savings plan and budget.

TOTAL INCOME: £50 (£15 ALLOWANCE + £35 WAGES)

| EXPENSES: | BUDGET | ACTUAL SPEND | DIFFERENCE |
|---|---|---|---|
| Travel | £10 | £8 | £2 |
| Phone contract | £15 | £15 | £0 |
| Food | £15 | £12 | £3 |
| Cinema | £10 | £8 | £2 |
| TOTAL: | £50 | £43 | £7 |

YOU HAVE £7 EXTRA TO SPEND OR SAVE.

I SAVE/INVEST FOR FUTURE GOALS, KEEP A PROPORTION FOR TIMES OF NEED AND I SPEND THE REST.

ANDY JEFFERIES, CO-FOUNDER OF DOCK & BAY — QUICK-DRYING TOWELS.

## WHERE SHOULD I PUT MY MONEY?

Keeping savings in a jar at home is OK, but there are ways to save money that will make you more money – now that sounds good, doesn't it!

There are lots of **saving accounts** out there for young people under the age of 18, and because banks and building societies want your money (so they can lend to others), they will pay you **interest** (*see page 74* for more info) – a reward for saving with them.

### DID YOU KNOW?

Let's compare saving money at home with a savings account giving 5% interest per year. How much money would you need to save each day to have £5,000 on your 25th birthday:

| From your . . . | In a jar | In a savings account paying 5% interest per year |
|---|---|---|
| 12th birthday | £1.06 | 74p |
| 15th birthday | £1.37 | £1.04 |
| 18th birthday | £1.96 | £1.61 |

## IS MY MONEY SAFE IN A BANK?

Pretty safe because it's the Bank of England's job to keep an eye on banks and there are rules and regulations to protect you. Nothing is guaranteed, though. Although it's rare, things can go wrong.

## WHAT HAPPENS IF A BANK GOES WRONG?

If it belongs to the **Financial Service Compensation Scheme (FSCS)**, then up to £85,000 of your money is protected or up to £170,000 if you share your account with someone (called a joint account). This limit is per bank.

## ARE ALL BANKS THE SAME?

Banks want your money and compete to win you over by offering a good interest rate. They will offer other things, too, sometimes even cash, so look around before you choose your bank. Not all banks are the same!

### DID YOU KNOW?

**Commercial banks** are the banks we use for everyday services, like paying wages into and withdrawing cash. **Investment banks** offer financial services to larger organisations and big investors (private and institutions).

## CHOOSING THE RIGHT ACCOUNT

There are lots of different types of savings accounts for under 18s. Let's get familiar with them to help you choose the right one for you:

- **EASY ACCESS SAVINGS ACCOUNTS**
  These let you put money in and take it out whenever you want.

- **NOTICE ACCOUNTS**
  You must tell the bank or building society if you want to take money out before you can do so (e.g. three months before you want it).

- **REGULAR SAVINGS ACCOUNTS**
  You must make regular payments and your money is typically locked away, usually for 12 months, or you have to pay a penalty. Some offer 1–3 free withdrawals a year.

That's a bit to get your head around, but as a rule, the longer you lock your money away, the more you will be paid for it.

**TO DECIDE WHICH ACCOUNT IS BEST FOR YOU, CHECK HOW MUCH INTEREST YOU WILL BE PAID AND THINK ABOUT WHEN YOU WILL NEED TO TAKE OUT YOUR MONEY.**

COMPARE INTEREST RATES BY LOOKING AT THE **AER** (ANNUAL EQUIVALENT RATE). THE HIGHER THE AER, THE MORE INTEREST YOU'LL RECEIVE FOR YOUR SAVINGS.

## HOW DO I OPEN A BANK ACCOUNT?

Between 11 and 15, you can open an account with the help of a parent or guardian. To open your own account, you need to be at least 16. You can either go into a bank to open an account or do it online.

## WHAT WILL I NEED TO OPEN A BANK ACCOUNT?

The bank will need your name, proof of where you live and that you are who you say you are (e.g. by showing your passport, driving licence or a birth certificate). They may want other things too – each bank is different.

### DID YOU KNOW?

You can help make banking simple with a **banking app** – it is a quick way to look at your account(s) and check your balance and spending. *See pages 78–79 for more info.*

## WHAT ABOUT SPENDING MONEY?

You will need a bank account, so you have money that is easy to get to, to pay bills, buy food, etc., and you will need somewhere to put your wages! This is a **current account**. There are loads of them and are mostly free, but most don't pay interest.

## HOW DO I CHOOSE A CURRENT ACCOUNT?

A current account might be free, but if you need extras, such as an overdraft (*see page 114*) or transferring money abroad, you'll have to pay **transaction fees**. Each bank will have its own list, so always check. The upside is that banks may offer goodies to win you over . . . even cash! So, compare what they charge and what they are giving you and see how it fits with what you want.

## WHAT'S THE DIFFERENCE BETWEEN A BANK AND A BUILDING SOCIETY?

The BIG difference is that banks are owned by shareholders and building societies are owned by and work for their customers. Why does that matter? Well, because building societies don't have to pay out some of their profit (called **dividends**) to shareholders, they sometimes offer better interest rates – so they're worth checking out!

## CHALLENGE: CAN YOU SAVE YOUR FAMILY MONEY?

Together with a parent or guardian, see if you can make some savings on the bills. Let's start with electricity – a bill most households pay monthly.

- Ask to have a look at the latest electricity bill to see what the current deal is.

- Go online and find three electricity companies and see what deals they offer. Write each one down and compare them to find out which one is the best. Have you found a better deal?

- Try again with other things . . . such as credit cards, mobile phones and internet services.

**WOULDN'T IT BE BRILLIANT IF YOU COULD SAVE YOUR FAMILY MONEY?**

## HOW DO I MAKE MY MONEY GROW?

Say you have found a bank that will pay 5% interest on your savings. You need to check if that is compound or simple interest.

**COMPOUND INTEREST** is interest on the money you have in your account, plus interest on the interest you have already received. Let me show you . . .

**TODAY:** You put £10 into your account.

**1 YEAR LATER:** You earned 5% interest on £10 (which is 50p) over the first year, so you now have £10.50.

**2 YEARS LATER:** You earned 5% interest on £10.50 (which is 52.5p) over the second year, so you now have £11.025. And your money keeps growing.

In real life, compound interest is usually calculated daily, monthly or quarterly, but this gives you the idea. The more often it is calculated, the faster your money grows.

**SIMPLE INTEREST** (at 5%) means that for the same £10 you would earn 50p each year, because you only ever earn 5% on the original amount you saved. Simples!

## HOW CAN I MAKE MY MONEY GROW FASTER?

Interest is one way of growing your money. **Investing** is another. That means buying things that are likely to go up in value over time, like antiques, property, shares and even trainers! This can be fun and rewarding, but also risky. If you invest in the wrong things, you can lose money, so doing research and understanding why something may grow in value before you hand your money over is important.

## HOW DO I DECIDE TO SAVE OR INVEST?

Investing can be risky. Think about it, if you have to sell an investment because you need to pay a big bill, it might be at a time when the investment is worth less than what you paid for it. If you think you will need the money in the near future, it is better to save it.

ONLY INVEST MONEY YOU CAN AFFORD TO LOSE AND <u>NEVER</u> MONEY YOU NEED TO LIVE.

## IS THERE A LIMIT ON HOW MUCH MONEY I CAN GET FROM A CASH MACHINE?

It depends on you and your bank, and you will be told this when you get your payment card (e.g. debit, credit, ATM cards). A daily limit is given for safety reasons – for you, for the bank and to stop people from being tricked by fraudsters and losing all their money. Your limit will be lower if your **credit score** is poor (*see page 120* for more details).

## WHAT IF I NEED MORE MONEY THAN THAT?

You can go into your bank, but even then, there will be limits to the amount you can take out instantly – check the limit so you don't have a wasted trip! If you want more, you must let them know in advance – for your protection and theirs.

## SHOULD I SWITCH BANKS?

Some banks may offer cash deals to switch your account to one of theirs, and it may be tempting to snap them up. But good service, support when you need it and shared values are all good reasons to stay loyal and not just jump for a short-term cash gain. If you are not getting the service or rates you want, though, that's different!

## WHAT WOULD HAPPEN IF WE ALL TOOK OUT OUR MONEY FROM BANKS AT THE SAME TIME?

Banks lend more money than they have – quite a lot more actually! They rely on us not wanting all our money at the same time and they are usually right. BUT, if people get spooked about the safety of their money, they can panic and rush to take out their cash. This is called a 'run on the banks' and can even lead to the bank collapsing.

### DID YOU KNOW?

One of the biggest bank runs of the 21st century happened quite recently when customers withdrew $42 billion in one day from Silicon Valley Bank, in the United States, in a panic whipped up by social media and viral posts. To prevent huge losses to businesses and individuals, the government stepped in to guarantee the money.

## HOW DOES ONLINE BANKING WORK?

You can use your computer or mobile phone to do just about everything you used to have to go into a bank for – perhaps you are already? Using your devices can help you budget because you can look at your account 24 hours a day. And if you need to pay for something urgently, you can.

## IS ONLINE BANKING SAFE?

Yes, BUT, be careful – because online banking is done remotely, it can be easier for people to trick you into paying them money or giving them your bank details or passwords, so they can pretend to be you and withdraw YOUR money. Don't use free Wi-Fi in public places to log in to your online account, because it isn't secure.

IF YOU LOSE YOUR PHONE OR LAPTOP, CONTACT YOUR BANK IMMEDIATELY TO STOP ANYONE USING YOUR INFORMATION TO SPEND YOUR MONEY!

## WHAT DIGITAL MONEY DATA IS GATHERED ONLINE?

Every time we buy online, information is gathered on us to help retailers understand what customers are buying and when they are buying them, for example, to help them build a picture of who their customers are and what we might want to buy, so they can sell us more stuff.

## BENEFITS OF ONLINE BANKING

- You can access your bank account from a smartphone, computer or tablet.

- It's possible to check your balance whenever you want to.

- Payments are quick and easy to make.

- Easy to see what money is coming in and going out.

- Simple to set up regular payments.

- Setting up alerts can tell you if the bank sees anything they think might be suspicious or can alert you to when you're running out of money.

## TOP TIPS TO STAY SAFE ONLINE

- Always **use a different secure password** for each app or website, and don't tell anyone what it is.

- **Change your passwords regularly** – maybe use password manager apps to help store your passwords and keep them safe.

- Make sure you **update your software and apps** regularly, so you have the latest security features.

If you get an email or text asking for your personal or bank details, be suspicious – companies won't ask for these details by email or text.

ALWAYS BE CAREFUL. IF IN DOUBT,
CHECK WITH YOUR BANK BY
VISITING THEIR WEBSITE OR
CALLING THEM DIRECTLY.

Here are some more things to check,
if you get a suspicious-looking email . . .

CHECK THE **EMAIL ADDRESS** IT WAS
SENT FROM. IS IT FROM THE BANK OR DOES
IT LOOK LIKE AN ODD ADDRESS, POSSIBLY
WITH LOTS OF RANDOM NUMBERS?

IS THE **DATE**
CORRECT?

DOES THE **LOGO**
LOOK EXACTLY LIKE
THE BANK LOGO AND IS
IT CRISP AND CLEAR?

HAVE THEY USED
YOUR **NAME**? IS IT
SPELT CORRECTLY?
ARE THERE ANY OTHER
DODGY **SPELLINGS**?

DON'T CLICK ON LINKS.

IS IT TRYING TO
PUSH YOU INTO DOING
SOMETHING **QUICKLY**?
SCAMMERS OFTEN DO THIS
TO TRY AND GET YOU TO
TAKE IMMEDIATE ACTION.

**From:** B@nk_1DeborahMeaden987
**Sent:** Saturday, September 7, 2024
**Subject:** URGENT – YOUR ACCOUNT

# bank

Dear Custmer,

Congratulations! We have an
exclusive offer just for you:

CLICK HERE NOW TO CLAIM!

You must reply in 24h or your
account will be closed.

Sincerely,
Joe Bloggs

## WHAT IS A PENSION?

A **pension** is a savings plan you build up over your working life, so you have money when you retire.

## AM I TOO YOUNG TO THINK ABOUT A PENSION?

It feels a bit odd thinking about finishing work when you've hardly started, but the earlier you start paying into a pension, the longer your money has to grow.

## HOW MUCH SHOULD I PAY INTO A PENSION?

It is up to you, but a good guide is around 12.5% of what you earn. Think about when you plan to retire, what you want to do and how much that will cost. Then find out how much you will get from your **state pension** and try to work out how much you will need to make up the difference. It's true things will cost more in the future, but there are online tools to help you work all that out.

## DO I GET ANY HELP WITH MY PENSION?

Your employer may contribute as part of your salary, and you may add to that. If you work for yourself, you may choose to pay regularly into your pension (money you pay in is tax-free to a certain limit and will get a top-up from the government).

## WHAT IF I HAVE TO STOP WORK BEFORE I GET MY PENSION?

There's support if you need it, such as care home nursing, NHS services and possibly money from the government, called **benefits**. And have you heard of **illness insurance**, sometimes called income protection insurance? You pay a regular sum, called a premium, to an insurance company, and if something happens to stop you working, they could pay you money to replace a salary or cover mortgage repayments, for example. It is something we all hope we will never need, but it is always worth thinking 'What IF something happens?'.

## DO I NEED LIFE INSURANCE?

This is a type of insurance that is paid out when you die – either in one payment or via regular payments. It's useful if people rely on you financially, and some mortgage lenders won't let you borrow money without having life insurance.

### DID YOU KNOW?

A form of life insurance has been around for thousands of years. The ancient Greeks and Romans formed 'benevolent societies' to cover funeral costs and support bereaved families.

## CAN I BE SNEAKY WITH MY MONEY?

You could, but should you? There are plenty of ways you can correctly reduce the amount you pay in tax and that may be OK. However, if we want everyone to be looked after, then we all have to pay towards that through taxes.

## WHAT IS AN OFFSHORE ACCOUNT?

A bank account in another country, not connected to the UK. There are good reasons why people have them, such as working abroad, as you need to keep your money locally – all perfectly legal. They get a bad name when people use them to hide their money to avoid paying tax, which is illegal.

## WHAT'S THE DIFFERENCE BETWEEN TAX EVASION AND TAX AVOIDANCE?

Well, tax evasion is when you hide income or information from HMRC and that is illegal. Tax avoidance is when you manage your finances in a way to reduce tax – legally!

A US ENTREPRENEUR WAS CONVICTED IN 2006 OF THE LARGEST TAX EVASION CASE IN US HISTORY – HE EVADED $200 MILLION IN TAX!

# CHAPTER 4

# SPENDING MONEY

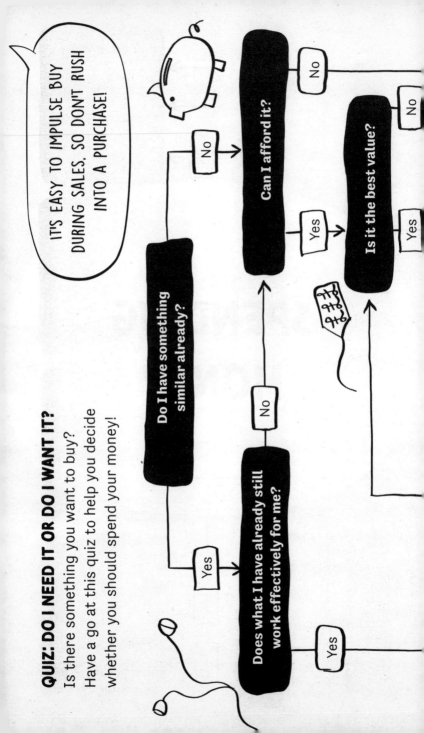

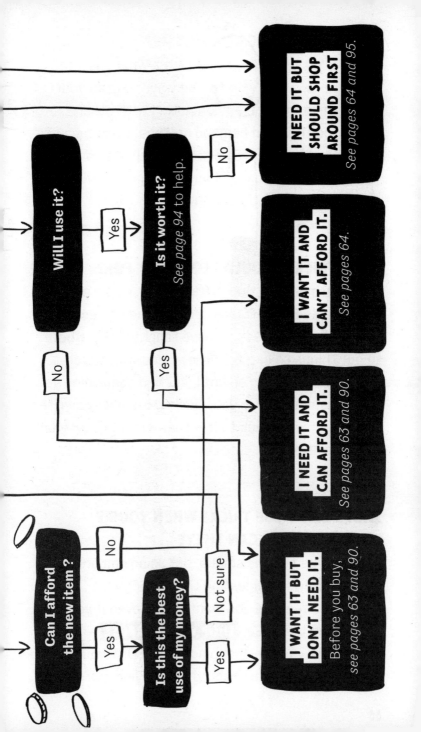

**Will I use it?**

No → **Is it worth it?**
*See page 94 to help.*

Yes →

**Is it worth it?**
No → **I NEED IT BUT SHOULD SHOP AROUND FIRST**
*See pages 64 and 95.*

Yes →

**I WANT IT AND CAN'T AFFORD IT.**
*See pages 64.*

**I NEED IT AND CAN AFFORD IT.**
*See pages 63 and 90.*

**Can I afford the new item?**

Yes → **Is this the best use of my money?**

No →

Not sure →

Yes → **I WANT IT BUT DON'T NEED IT.**
*Before you buy, see pages 63 and 90.*

## ARE SHOPS TRYING TO TRICK ME?

Shops want to sell you stuff – it's what they do!
They are always trying to find ways to grab your
attention, and they are competing with other
shops too. This can be good and bad. Good because
they will offer you free or cheaper things to win
your custom, but bad because you may be tricked
into buying stuff you don't need.

## WHAT TRICKS SHOULD I LOOK OUT FOR?

Offers are not the only trick! Colour, music and
even smells like coffee or fresh bread can entice
you. And years of selling have taught shops where
to put things to catch your eye! You won't even
notice what's going on until you find something you
didn't mean to buy in your basket! So, always write
a list and try to stick to it – that way you buy what
you actually want.

## SHOPS CAN'T USE TRICKS WHEN YOU'RE BUYING ONLINE, CAN THEY?

Well, maybe not the smells, but using colours,
online reviews, suggesting things for you . . . all
makes you feel like you want things even if you
don't need them. So, **SHOP WITH PURPOSE** – always
know what you are shopping for BEFORE you start
and try not to be distracted into buying more.

# INTERVIEW WITH
# BETH CHILTON

Owner of women's fashion brand Hope & Ivy

## ARE YOU A SPENDER OR A SAVER?

I'm both. At the beginning of each month, I put
a proportion into a savings account and then I split
the balance into four weekly spending amounts.
If I have any money left over at the end of each
week I indulge in a small treat! Or I collect this
together for an end-of-month big treat!

## WHAT ARE YOUR TOP MONEY SAVING TIPS?

My savings are with different providers to my
current account, so there is no temptation to dip
into the savings pot. And I have always used ISAs*
and shopped around for those with the
best interest rates.

## WHAT IS YOUR BEST AND WORST PURCHASE?

Best is a designer bag (I work in fashion!) and
worst is all clothing I purchased in my early 20s.

*Individual Savings Accounts – where you can save or invest
money (currently up to £20,000 per tax year) tax-free. Over
16s can open a cash ISA and over-18s can open a stocks
and shares ISA. Junior ISAs are available for under-18s –
currently up to £9,000 can be saved or invested per tax year.

# MONEY SAVING TIPS

- Know what you want to buy. **Start with a list**.

- **Don't buy something you hadn't planned to** just because it is 'on sale' or part of an offer.

- **Shop around**. If online, use price-checking sites.

- Do your own **research**. Use independent-review sites, not just the ones the shops show you.

- **Don't be tempted by special 'add-ons'** at the checkout.

- **Never be rushed into a quick decision**. Always check other shops for the best prices.

- **Look out for hidden costs** like delivery and compare TOTAL costs with other shops.

- Wear a nose peg so you can't smell the fresh bread. Just kidding! But do **be aware of the tricks**!

## HOW MUCH COULD YOU SAVE?

Pick something you buy often, such as a can of drink, and when you visit a shop, café or vending machine, write down how much it costs. At the end of the month check the difference between the cheapest and most expensive. See how much you could save by shopping around!

# INTERVIEW WITH
# PROF. ANUSHA SHAH

President – Institution of Civil Engineers and
Senior Director – Resilient Cities, Arcadis

## WHAT LED YOU TO DO THE JOB YOU HAVE NOW?

Being clear on my purpose: bringing people and
solutions together that benefit people and nature.
I find it hugely uplifting.

## WHAT MONEY ADVICE WOULD YOU GIVE TO YOUR TEENAGE SELF?

Growing up, my parents' singular focus was on me
getting an education, which is great, but I wish
I had also been empowered to take up part-time
jobs, earn money, understand the value of money
and get comfortable with building wealth. I would
advise my teenage self that money is an important
enabler for doing many things we enjoy, so start
earning, saving and investing.

## ARE YOU A SPENDER OR A SAVER?

I was a spender until I started saving to buy my
first home. That got me into a habit of saving to
invest in something that brings comfort and joy.

## BEST PRICE VS BEST VALUE FOR MONEY

Sometimes products can seem cheaper than others, but look closely, it may not be as simple as it first seems . . .

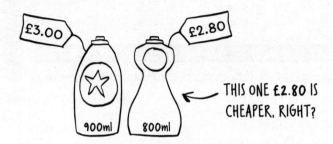

£3.00

£2.80

900ml  800ml

THIS ONE £2.80 IS CHEAPER, RIGHT?

Well, it costs less, but is it the best value? The bottles look a similar size, but if you work out the price per 100ml, the £3.00 bottle is better value.

**£3.00 divided by 9 = 33p for each 100ml**
**£2.80 divided by 8 = 35p for each 100ml**

DIVIDE BY THE NUMBER OF 100ML UNITS IN THE BOTTLE.

Shops usually have the price per unit on the price label, but if not, you can now work it out yourself.

BUYING THINGS IN A GREATER VOLUME CAN BE BETTER VALUE, BUT NOT ALWAYS, SO DON'T FORGET TO CHECK!

## CHALLENGE

which packet of pasta is the best value?

- 500g one for 75p (£1.50/kg)
- 400g one for 70p (£1.75/kg)
- 1kg one for £1.40 (£1.40/kg)

Answer: 1kg

## WHY DO THINGS GO ON SALE?

When shops have too much of something, they often want to sell it quickly e.g. when seasons change or things, like food, are going out of date. They'd rather sell it cheaply than throw it away. Or it happens when a business needs to raise cash quickly.

## ARE BLACK FRIDAY DEALS WORTH IT?

Black Friday started in the US, as the day the Christmas shopping season begins. It seems to offer amazing discounts, but are they really? If you were going to buy it anyway, then you may save money, but if not then it's probably a waste of money.

ACCORDING TO WHICH MAGAZINE, IN 2022, 98% OF BLACK FRIDAY DEALS WERE THE SAME PRICE OR CHEAPER AT OTHER TIMES OF THAT YEAR.

## HOW DO I NEGOTIATE?

Not everything can or should be negotiated, but sometimes it's OK! If you find something you know is cheaper elsewhere (be honest), you could ask if a shop could match the price. Or if buying in bulk (perhaps clubbing together with friends), or if something has a flaw or is out of your budget, then perhaps ask for discount. It's up to the shop whether they say yes or no!

Here are some tips so it goes well, even if you don't get what you hoped for.

- Do **research** so you can explain how much you will pay and why.

- **Find the person who can negotiate** (e.g. the manager/owner), not everyone can.

- **Stay calm and friendly**.

- If they offer something else (such as a different model), **take time to consider**.

- **Be prepared to walk away.**

## IS IT WORTH BUYING?

This isn't just down to the price, but also the **value** (what something is worth to someone). Value means different things to different people (e.g. someone might value the environment and pay more for something that is plastic-free).

## MAKE YOUR MONEY GO FURTHER
Look for the best deal or value
(which is not always the best price).

- Find **discount codes** or discount vouchers to spend on the things you need.

- Keep your eye on something you can't afford, it might go on **sale**.

- Items with slight **imperfections** or that have been used for display are often discounted.

- Buy things **out of season**. Christmas cards in January can be a bargain!

- Check out **short-date food and drink**, shops often sell them cheap.

- Visit **outlet shops**, they often have lovely stuff at lower prices.

- Buy **preloved items** or **swap** with a friend.

- For special occasions, when you might just wear something once, consider **renting** your outfit.

# FUN ON A BUDGET

Surprise your family or friends by planning something fun on budget. What could you do for under £5 or £10? Use your imagination. Here are some ideas to get you started:

- Pack up a picnic and plan a nature walk or a city walk.

- Find out some interesting facts about where you live and act as a tour guide or visit a museum.

- Look out for free events locally.

- Bring together all your beauty products and create your own spa.

- Bake some treats or make popcorn and choose a movie to watch.

- Have a board game evening — maybe pick up one from a second-hand shop. You could buy small treats for the winners!

- Cook a meal. Search online for recipes or borrow cookery books from the library.

# INTERVIEW WITH
# TANYA STEELE

Chief Executive, WWF-UK
(World Wide Fund for Nature)

## WHAT'S YOUR BEST AND WORST PURCHASE?

Best is my bike . . . I've had it for 25 years.
Worst is gold platform shoes.

## ARE YOU A SPENDER OR A SAVER?

A spender. I have to work really hard at saving and
resist my two favourite items: shoes and books.

## WHAT WAS YOUR FIRST JOB?

On a supermarket checkout.

## WHAT DO YOU LOVE ABOUT YOUR CURRENT JOB?

I meet an incredible range of people who do
so much for wildlife and our natural world:
schoolchildren, youth activists, scientists,
politicians, business leaders, local and
indigenous communities, even the King. It gives
me enormous hope that we can save our planet.

## WHAT IS YOUR TOP MONEY SAVING TIP?

Whenever you receive money as a gift, save it –
you'll be surprised at how quickly it grows.

## WHAT IF I CHANGE MY MIND ABOUT SOMETHING I BUY?

You get swept away buying something and then change your mind when you get it home. We've all done it! What do you do? Well, it depends on where you bought it . . .

## WHAT HAPPENS IF I RETURN SOMETHING TO A SHOP?

If there's nothing wrong with it, then it's up to the shop. They don't have to give your money back. Shops have different terms and conditions, so check with them before you buy. And you can always check these by looking at the receipt, visiting their website or calling to ask.

If they won't refund you, they might let you swap it for something else or give you a **credit note** (a piece of paper or electronic copy you can use to buy something for the same amount later, usually before a set date). Or they might do nothing!

YOU WILL HAVE A BETTER CHANCE OF GETTING A REFUND IF YOU RETURN SOMETHING QUICKLY WITH THE RECEIPT AND ORIGINAL PACKAGING.

## WHAT IF I BOUGHT SOMETHING ONLINE?

Ah, now that's different. You hadn't seen the goods when you bought them, so you have up to 14 days from the day you receive your goods to decide to keep them or not. This is called a **cooling-off period**. If you change your mind, tell the shop. You then have another 14 days to send them back for a full refund (which includes the cost of standard delivery if you have paid for it). Unless the retailer says they will pay for returns, you'll have to pay the return postage. **Check a company's returns policy before purchasing online.**

WE ALL MAKE MISTAKES – I ONCE BOUGHT A CUP ONLINE AND WHEN IT TURNED UP IT WAS FOR A DOLL'S HOUSE!

## DO I HAVE 14 DAYS TO THINK ABOUT EVERYTHING I BUY ONLINE?

No, not if you buy from a private individual, say from a social media marketplace or online auction site. Some things don't have a cooling-off period either, for safety reasons or if they deteriorate quickly, like flowers, or because they have been made especially for you. However, they have to tell you this before you buy – it's the law!

## WHAT IF SOMETHING I BUY IS FAULTY?

Tell the business as soon as you know. If it's within 30 days from the date it arrived, they have to give you your money back. After 30 days, they can repair it and not give you a refund (although it's always worth asking!). After six months, it is tricky because you will have to prove the fault was there when you bought it, and that can be hard!

> DON'T PANIC IF YOUR FAULTY ITEM DOESN'T HAVE A RECEIPT – SHOW PROOF OF PAYMENT, FOR EXAMPLE, A BANK STATEMENT.

## CAN I ALWAYS GET MY MONEY BACK IF I LET THEM KNOW OF A FAULT WITHIN 30 DAYS?

Not if you knew about the fault when you bought it. Usually, the shop will make it clear on the receipt that it is non-returnable.

## WHAT IF I BUY SOMETHING FROM ABROAD?

Each country has its own rules, and they might not protect you in the same way as buying from the UK, so always check a seller's terms and conditions to make sure you are happy buying from them.

IF YOU PAY FOR PURCHASES THAT
COST BETWEEN £100 AND £30,000
WITH A CREDIT CARD, YOU GET
PURCHASE PROTECTION.

FOR EXAMPLE, IF THE ITEM DOESN'T TURN
UP OR THE RETAILER GOES OUT OF BUSINESS,
YOU MAY GET YOUR MONEY BACK THROUGH
YOUR CREDIT CARD COMPANY.

## WHAT IS INSURANCE?

Insurance is like a safety net. It protects you by
paying you money if the unexpected happens.
Say you have insured an expensive phone and you
lose it, you call up the insurance company and
they check a few things. They may agree to pay
for a new one, but not necessarily all of it! To
stop you making lots of little claims there is an
'**excess**', which means an amount you will have
to pay towards the cost of replacing or repairing
something. It is there to make you stop and think
about whether to claim or not to claim!

## HOW DOES INSURANCE WORK?

When people pay an insurance company, the money
goes into a 'pool' to pay out from if needed. As
many people won't make a claim, the insurance
companies get to keep the rest of the money!

## WHAT SHOULD I INSURE?

You can insure anything that has value and is important to you. A phone, a house, valuable jewellery, even your legs if you are a brilliant football player! Some things you have to insure by law, such as cars, because if you damage someone else's property with your car, you must be able to pay for the repairs.

Questions to ask yourself to help you decide whether to insure an item . . .

- How much would it cost to replace?
- How likely am I to lose or break it?
- Is it likely that someone will steal it?
- How much will I have to pay to insure it?

## IS INSURANCE EXPENSIVE?

That depends. The less likely something is to happen, the cheaper it is. The price also depends on the value of what's being insured. Bank accounts can sometimes include free insurance in packages. And if your family has home contents insurance, check what this covers.

## WHERE DO I BUY INSURANCE?

Lots of people sell insurance, you only have to look online to see how many. You usually buy through an online comparison site, and they can help you choose by comparing different offers called 'quotes'.

> SOME SHOPS ALSO SELL INSURANCE FOR SMALL ELECTRICAL ITEMS — ACCIDENTAL DAMAGE COVER, FOR EXAMPLE.

## WHAT HAPPENS NEXT?

Once you've chosen an insurer, fill out a **proposal**, which asks lots of questions. Tell the truth because they use this to decide if they will insure you. They then **quote** how much it will cost and tell you exactly what they will cover and for how long. If you accept the quote, you pay your money (a **premium**) and . . . you are insured! You then get a record of this – your insurance policy.

> FOOTBALL LEGEND MESSI HAD HIS LEFT FOOT INSURED FOR 750 MILLION EUROS.

## HOW CAN I AFFORD TO MOVE OUT?

Renting can be a great first step and there are loads of options. You can club together with friends and share the costs to rent a place, find a smaller place to rent by yourself or rent a room in a shared house. It is all about how much you can afford – don't forget to include money for any extra bills in your budget.

When I first moved out of my parents' house, I lived in a youth hostel in Brighton – it was a lot of fun sharing a place and it was cheap!

## HOW DO I KNOW HOW MUCH RENT I CAN AFFORD?

It is different for everyone, but a guide is not to pay more than one third of your gross salary (salary before tax or anything is taken out). To work that out:

Divide your yearly salary by 3 = yearly rent
Then divide your yearly rent by 12 = monthly rent

The question is, what can YOU afford? Put the monthly number into your budget along with all the bills you will have to pay and see if you have enough money to cover everything (including some money to have a good time!).

## WHAT ELSE WILL I HAVE TO PAY IF I RENT?

Ah, that's a good question because each place is different and to find that out you need to ask questions like . . .

- Who pays for **council tax** and **home insurance**?

- Are **bills**, such as electricity and water, included in the rent?

- Are there any **service charges** (things the property owner might pay for and charge you)?

- Do I need to pay for a **TV licence** and **internet**?

- Does it come **furnished** or **unfurnished**?

- Is there **anything else** not included in the rent?

DON'T FORGET, YOU'LL NEED TO PAY FOR
FOOD, TRANSPORT, PERSONAL SPENDING,
ANY DEBT PAYMENTS AND SAVINGS.

## HOW DO I REMEMBER ALL THOSE PAYMENTS?

That is a lot of stuff to juggle, but there are ways to make it easier. Here are some of them. First up, **budget** (*see page 62*). Remember, budgets need to be kept up-to-date to really help you.

You can spread big payments over time and even save money by using automatic payments because some companies give you a discount for doing this.

## WHAT ARE AUTOMATIC PAYMENTS?

**DIRECT DEBITS** tell the bank that the company you are paying can take your money automatically. It is good for regular bills from trusted organisations and when the amount changes, like electricity bills. If there are any mistakes or wrong payments, your bank guarantees to give your money back.

A **STANDING ORDER** might be better if the amount is always the same and to the same person/company. Tell your bank how much to pay, how often and to whom. You are in control of the payments.

Include any automatic payments in your budget and if you don't know exactly what a bill will be, have a good guess. It's better than getting into trouble by missing it altogether!

ALWAYS CHECK YOUR BANK STATEMENTS TO SEE IF THEY AGREE WITH YOUR BUDGET. THAT WAY YOU CAN SPOT MISTAKES AND KNOW WHEN YOU NEED TO CHANGE YOUR BUDGET.

## WHAT IF I CAN'T PAY MY BILLS?

It's very worrying, but there is help around and getting help sooner is better. If you can't pay a bill, speak to the organisation as soon as there is a problem and ask for help – perhaps giving you more time to pay or reducing monthly payments.

## I HAVE FOUND SOMEWHERE I CAN AFFORD TO RENT, NOW WHAT DO I DO?

How exciting! Now, to stop anyone else getting it, you might need to pay a **holding deposit** (up to a week's rent for the property). You'll get this back unless you change your mind, or give wrong or misleading information. You must also prove you can pay the rent – the property owner will check your **credit score** (see page 120), to check if you are financially reliable. And you need someone to vouch for you. This process is called a **reference** and is usually a previous person you're rented from. If you haven't rented before, ask your employer for a reference.

## WHEN WILL I PAY MY FIRST RENT?

Before you move in, you'll usually need to have enough money to pay for a month's rent in advance, plus a **tenancy deposit** (usually another month's rent that is kept by a third party).

## WHY DO I HAVE TO PAY A TENANCY DEPOSIT?

In case you miss a rent payment or leave the place damaged or dirty. If everything is fine you will get it back when you leave, but if not, the property owner might keep some/it all. To help avoid disputes, take photos when you leave and get your landlord to sign a check-in and check-out inventory.

> YOUR DEPOSIT MUST BE PUT IN A GOVERNMENT—APPROVED TENANCY DEPOSIT SCHEME (TDP) BY THE PROPERTY OWNER.

## WHAT IF I CAN'T MAKE A RENT PAYMENT?

Check your budget, work out when you will be able to pay and speak to the property owner. They don't have to agree to anything though, and if you keep doing it or are past the end date of your tenancy agreement, they can start an eviction process to remove you from the property, meaning you could end up with nowhere to live.

## WHAT IS A TENANCY AGREEMENT?

It is a contract between you and the property owner. A written one is best because it is easy to forget or misunderstand what has been said.

IF YOU ARE HAVING PROBLEMS PAYING RENT, ALWAYS SPEAK TO THE PEOPLE INVOLVED. THEY MAY BE ABLE TO HELP AND IGNORING THINGS ALWAYS MAKES THEM WORSE!

# INTERVIEW WITH
# A RENTER

Elizabeth, age 29, has been in the private rental market for six years, with a few breaks staying with family in between contracts.

### WHAT ARE THE GOOD BITS ABOUT RENTING?

It's a good way to explore different areas without committing to buying, and it's helpful not having to shoulder the expense if things go wrong with your house. I've been lucky though and have always had good property owners who fix things promptly – this is definitely not the case for everyone.

### ARE THERE ANY BAD BITS ABOUT RENTING?

Finding properties is stressful! Good rental properties go super quickly, you often have to make a snap decision, and finding places with move dates that line up is very hard. It's also very expensive, especially in London – I've moved further out where I can get more for my money.

### WOULD YOU LIKE TO BUY A HOUSE ONE DAY?

Yes – my partner and I are exploring areas and saving up for a deposit, but it's not easy with the high cost of living.

## HOUSES COST A LOT. HOW DO I PAY FOR ONE?

Most people don't have enough money to pay for a whole house upfront, so they get a **mortgage** (a type of loan, usually from a building society or bank), that is paid back over time.

There are lots of different types of mortgage. Here's a quick guide to some of them:

- **REPAYMENT MORTGAGE:** You pay back some of the money you have borrowed each month PLUS interest on the loan, so over time you pay back all of the house cost, plus extra for the interest.

- **INTEREST-ONLY MORTGAGE:** You only pay the interest on the loan, so the payments look lower, but you're only paying the interest on the loan and not the amount you originally borrowed (called the capital).

- **FIXED-RATE MORTGAGE:** Interest rates usually go up and down, but if you agree a fixed rate, then they stay at that level for an agreed length of time (often two, three or five years from when the mortgage starts).

- **STANDARD VARIABLE-RATE MORTGAGE:** The repayments can change, usually as interest rates change. This can make it hard to budget, as interest rates can change a lot depending on how the country is doing financially. There are different types, e.g. tracker mortgages.

## CAN I BORROW ALL THE MONEY TO BUY A HOUSE?

Unlikely. You'll probably need to make up the difference with something called a **deposit**. A deposit is usually between 5% and 20% of the house price. So, if your house is £200,000, you will need between £10,000 and £40,000. That's a lot of money to save!

## WHAT HAPPENS IF I MISS A MORTGAGE PAYMENT?

If it's the first time, your mortgage company will probably be pretty helpful, so don't panic! Look at your budget and work out what has happened. It may be just a blip. If you can afford to pay a little more over the next few months, ring your mortgage company and agree a plan. You might have to spend less on the things you want for a while but it is worth it, because if you keep missing payments, they can take ownership of your house and sell it to get the money you owe them.

I HAD TO SELL MY FIRST HOUSE WHEN INTEREST RATES ROCKETED TO 17% AND I COULDN'T MAKE MY MONTHLY PAYMENTS. I SAW IT COMING THOUGH, SO HAD SAVED SOME MONEY TO GIVE ME TIME TO SELL.

# INTERVIEW WITH A HOMEOWNER

First-time buyer Sean, age 31, bought his home in 2023.

## WHAT ARE THE GOOD BITS ABOUT OWNING A HOME?

Buying a house gives you complete freedom over the space you call home. Want to tear out a carpet or paint a wall? No problem, it's yours to do as you please! I also like that I'm no longer paying off someone else's mortgage. (Rent is usually the cost of the property owner's mortgage plus profit.)

## ARE THERE BAD BITS ABOUT OWNING A HOME?

You're responsible for its upkeep, e.g. if the boiler stops working, then you've got to foot the bill. It feels like these problems occur more often than when I was renting, but this might just be because I've started paying more attention now that I'm responsible for the costs.

## WHAT ARE YOUR TOP TIPS?

Do your research and take time to find a good solicitor to help you understand the paperwork and the house-buying process.

# CHAPTER 5

## BORROWING MONEY

# POSSIBLE BORROWING OPTIONS

There are plenty of places you can borrow money, but you need to know how much you need, how long you need it for, how much it costs to borrow and how and when you will be able to pay it back.

## PERSONAL LOANS

Good for borrowing a fixed amount of money that is paid back over a set period, with interest added. Check if it is **compound** or **simple interest**.

LOAN INTEREST IS SHOWN AS AN APR (ANNUAL PERCENTAGE RATE), WHICH INCLUDES ALL THE COSTS, TO HELP YOU COMPARE OFFERS.

## OVERDRAFTS (OVER-18S ACCOUNTS ONLY)

This allows you to take more money out of your current account than you have, up to an agreed amount. The bank may just give you one, or you might have to ask. Interest may be charged, which is usually higher than taking out a loan, so they can be expensive and are best used short term.

IF YOU ACCIDENTALLY SPEND MORE THAN YOUR 'ARRANGED' OVERDRAFT, THIS IS CALLED AN 'UNARRANGED' OVERDRAFT. YOU WILL HAVE TO PAY FOR IT, AND IT MAY AFFECT YOUR CREDIT SCORE.

## CREDIT CARDS

If you need to buy something now and can afford to pay the money back before the end of the month, paying with a credit card may be a good choice. You won't have to pay interest and can improve your credit score. However, if you don't pay on time, it can be costly and give a bad credit score!

**CREDIT CARDS HAVE A HIGHER APR THAN BANK LOANS.**

## HIRE PURCHASE (HP)

If you want to buy something expensive, you may be offered HP. You'd pay a deposit and then a monthly fee, plus interest, for an agreed period, which can end up costing a lot more than the original price. And it isn't yours until the final payment is made. If you don't pay, they can take it away.

### CHALLENGE
which loan would be best to buy a . . .

1: £50 top (to repay by the end of the month)?
2: £500 laptop (to repay over two months)?

Answers: 1 = credit card.
2 = personal loan or overdraft.

## WHAT ARE CREDIT UNIONS?

They are a bit like a club where members 'pool' their savings to offer other members credit at a low interest rate. However, you must be a member and there are lots of rules. For instance, you may have to be part of an organisation or live in a certain area.

## WHAT IS PEER-TO-PEER LENDING?

People lending to each other direct without banks being involved. Online platforms help with this by matching lenders to borrowers, setting the interest rate and terms, and tracking loan repayments. Most UK platforms have a rule that you must be 18 before you join them.

## I SEE A LOT OF 'BUY NOW, PAY LATER' OFFERS, ARE THEY OK?

These pop up everywhere and are a way to spread the cost of something. Some charge interest, but many don't because the shops want you to buy from them, so they pay it. If you have your money planning right, these can be a good choice. However, always work out if you can make the payments before you buy, because if you miss them, you will pay a penalty AND it will affect your **credit score** (*see page 120*).

UK LENDERS SHOULD BE AUTHORISED BY THE FINANCIAL CONDUCT AUTHORITY (FCA), SO ALWAYS CHECK THEY HAVE A LICENCE FIRST. IT IS ILLEGAL TO LEND WITHOUT ONE.

## HOW CAN I GET MONEY REALLY QUICKLY?

Do you really need it? Short-term loans are often very expensive and can be the first step into bad debt (*see page 122*). And before you go down this route, ask yourself: Will I have cash to pay it back quickly? Where will the money come from? Will it leave me short next month?

### DOORSTEP LOANS

Someone comes to your door and offers to lend you money. Although it is usually small amounts, they are expensive as interest rates are very high.

### PAYDAY LOANS

These are easy to get online or in some high-street shops but are very expensive. You will be expected to pay them back when you get your next salary.

ILLEGAL MONEYLENDERS ('LOAN SHARKS') CHARGE VERY HIGH INTEREST AND RAISE RATES WHEN THEY WANT TO. THEY MAY EVEN USE ILLEGAL METHODS TO GET THEIR MONEY BACK.

## WHAT'S A STUDENT LOAN?

If you choose to go to university or college, you can apply for a loan from the **Student Loans Company (SLC)**, a government-funded organisation. The earliest you START to repay your student loan is from the April after you finish your course, but only once you're earning over a certain amount (the amount depends on your repayment plan). If you have a salaried job, paid for by your employer, this is taken out of your salary automatically (see payslip on *page 41*). Payments pause if you stop working or your income goes below the threshold for your repayment plan.

## WHAT IS A STUDENT LOAN USED FOR?

A **tuition fee loan** is for paying the costs of the course training, which usually goes straight to the university or college. A **maintenance costs loan** can be used to help with the cost of living and is paid directly to the student. How much, or even whether you can borrow from them, depends on how much money you or your household has.

## DO I HAVE TO PAY INTEREST ON A STUDENT LOAN?

Yes, it is still a loan even if it is a bit different. You will start building up interest (called accruing) from the moment your loan starts . . . even when you are studying. Whilst studying, the interest rate is the **RPI** (which stands for Retail Price Index and is the rate prices rise) plus 3%. After that the interest rate depends on your annual earnings. You also have to start paying the loan back every month once you are earning over a certain amount. How much you pay back each month depends on how much you are earning.

FOR STUDENT LOANS TAKEN OUT FROM 2023, ANY UNPAID STUDENT LOAN MONEY IS CANCELLED AFTER 40 YEARS.

## WHAT IS A CREDIT SCORE?

It is a number that tells people you want to borrow from how good you are with your money.

## DOES MY CREDIT SCORE MATTER?

Oooh, it matters a lot! The higher your score, the more likely you are to be able to borrow, pay less interest and be offered a credit card and other types of credit. You will also have a better chance of being able to rent than someone with a bad score. The lower your score gets, the more you are likely to pay if you need to borrow, and if it gets too low, you are unlikely to be able to borrow anything.

## WHO WORKS OUT MY CREDIT SCORE?

Credit ratings agencies. Some lenders even have their own departments to provide credit score information! Different companies might give different ratings, as they work it out differently, but things like late payments, too much money on credit cards and missing loan repayments will lower your score.

## HOW CAN I IMPROVE A LOW CREDIT SCORE?

Paying bills and rent on time, borrowing less and reducing debt will help change the picture.

## WHAT'S THE DIFFERENCE BETWEEN A CREDIT CARD AND A DEBIT CARD?

Quite a lot! When you spend on a credit card, you are actually borrowing money and if you don't pay it all off at the end of the month, you will pay interest. When you spend on a debit card, you are spending your own money because the bank takes the money straight from your account.

## WHAT ABOUT A PREPAID CARD?

A prepaid card is linked to your bank account. You put, or 'load', money onto the card, which you can then spend when you want to. It's a way of helping you control your money, because you can't usually spend more than you have loaded onto the card.

## HOW MANY CREDIT CARDS SHOULD I HAVE WHEN I'M OLDER?

Credit cards can be handy if used properly, BUT the money you are spending is 'invisible' and can be easy to lose track of. The more cards you have, the harder keeping track can be. And having too many can lower your credit score, as it may look like you are struggling with money.

## CAN I JUST PAY THE MINIMUM INTEREST ON CREDIT CARDS OR LOANS?

You can, but do you want to? You pay interest on anything you borrow, so it is cheaper to pay off more if you can afford to.

## WHAT'S DEBT?

It is something that is owed. It can be money, a favour, a service or goods. Let's talk about the money bit here. **MONEY DEBT CAN BE GOOD OR BAD!**

## HOW CAN DEBT BE GOOD?

If you borrow money that you know you can pay back and that can add lasting value to your life, debt can help you in a positive way. For example, to buy a bike so you can get to your new job or a house you can live in.

## SO HOW CAN DEBT BE BAD?

If you can't afford to pay back the money you borrow and you have spent it on things that lose their value quickly, such as gadgets or expensive clothes, that's bad debt.

## WHAT IS A DEBT SPIRAL?

If you keep borrowing, your debt gets bigger.
Then you have to keep borrowing more to pay
for the debt. If you feel worried and out of control,
it may be a debt spiral. How do you get out of it?

- Write a list of all your debt.

- Check your budget to see if you can reduce
  your costs or increase your income.

- Stop any impulse buying and don't increase
  your debt.

- Ask for help from those you are in debt to
  and/or a debt advisor.

## GOOD DEBT VS BAD DEBT

Check if you can see the difference between good debt and bad debt. What do you think about these situations?

1: Ella buys lots of stuff on her credit card, which she pays off every month. Good or bad debt?

2: Troy buys new games on his credit card and pays off the minimum amount he can each month. He pays interest on the money he hasn't paid off. Good or bad debt?

HAVE A SYSTEM IN PLACE TO PAY MONEY BACK BEFORE YOU BORROW — HAVE A PLAN FOR YOUR REPAYMENTS AND REMEMBER TO BUDGET!

Answers: 1 = Good debt because she isn't paying any interest. 2 = Bad debt because he is paying interest and games are a 'want' rather than a 'need'.

# CHAPTER 6

# STARTING YOUR OWN BUSINESS

## IDEAS, IDEAS, IDEAS

The best business ideas come from fixing a problem or making something better in some way . . . whether that is easier, cheaper, more environmentally friendly or just more beautiful! If you can come up with an idea that enough people want and you can provide at a price they will pay, then BOOM!, you are in business.

I NEVER QUITE FITTED INTO THE SCHOOL SYSTEM. I FOUND IT HARD TO PAY ATTENTION – IN PART BECAUSE OF MY ADHD. BUSINESS OFFERED A DIFFERENT AVENUE: IT PROVIDED THE FREEDOM TO CREATE MY OWN WORLD, BE MY OWN 'BOSS', EARN MONEY FROM THINGS I WOULD DO FOR FUN, AND A PATH TO TURN MY NEVER-ENDING LIST OF IDEAS INTO A REALITY.

STEVEN BARTLETT, ENTREPRENEUR

## HOW DO I COME UP WITH AN IDEA?

Keep your eyes open for something you can solve, do better or convince people they need. For example, if you see loads of people buying something on holiday you have never seen before, think if it would sell elsewhere.

Brainstorm with family and friends about things they need or problems they see. Do your research, go onto review sites and see if there are common complaints with a product that you can solve. There are opportunities all around, you just need to know them when you see them!

## YOU DON'T ALWAYS NEED A BRAND-NEW IDEA.

MOTOROLA INC. CAME UP WITH THE FIRST WIDELY USED MOBILE PHONES, BUT THEY WERE BIG, HEAVY AND CUMBERSOME. COMPETITORS THOUGHT 'WHAT A BRILLIANT IDEA!' THE PHONES WERE — THEY FIXED THE PROBLEMS AND MADE LIGHTER, SMALLER AND PRETTIER PHONES!

# INTERVIEW WITH
# STEVEN BARTLETT

Entrepreneur, podcast host, author and
youngest-ever dragon on *Dragons' Den*

## HOW DO YOU KNOW IF A BUSINESS WILL WORK?

The truth is, you don't know! Get started as soon
as you realistically can and focus on getting
feedback from the world about what you're doing.
It's very rare for anyone's initial business idea to
work perfectly. The best entrepreneurs change,
tweak, and alter their businesses constantly based
on customer feedback. You should hear all the
feedback, but you don't have to listen to all of it.
It's your job to decide which feedback is worth
implementing and which feedback is not important.

## HOW DO YOU DEAL WITH SETBACKS?

Every entrepreneur I have ever met has had
difficult days, big setbacks, criticism and moments
of self-doubt. Even the tallest mountains can be
climbed if you take one step at a time, are patient
with yourself, and you're being driven forward by
real passion. My dreams, ambition and self-belief
have fortunately remained bigger than any hurdle;
that's why setbacks haven't set me back.

## WHAT SKILLS DO I NEED TO SET UP A BUSINESS?

People skills! Don't underestimate the importance of being kind, likeable, listening to others, doing the right thing (even when nobody is watching!) and treating people well. If you're a good, kind person, people will lift you up, do favours for you and help you, and that can be the difference between success and failure in business and life!

## WHAT ARE YOUR TOP THREE TIPS?

**1. Dream even bigger!** If I had dreamed even bigger when I was younger, I would have failed even bigger, and failure is feedback, feedback is knowledge and knowledge is your power!

**2. Take a finance and investing course.** If you want to be successful in business, you're going to need at least a basic understanding of finance. And an advanced understanding of finance will give you a huge competitive advantage in business.

**3. Practise public speaking at a young age.** Knowing how to speak in front of people, in order to sell yourself or your ideas, is so important. Nobody starts out good at public speaking; you have to practise to get good at it!

## SHOULD I START MY OWN BUSINESS?

Business is selling something for a profit. It can be just one person doing it or lots of people. It can be big and complicated, such as technology company Apple Inc., which employs 161,000 people (as of 2023), or simple! Does that sound like something you want to do, or you might even be doing already?

## WHAT ARE THE BENEFITS?

I WOULD SAY THAT, WOULDN'T I?

Having your own business can be brilliant. You get to make your own decisions, choose what you want to do and how you want to do it and help others too, because if you are successful and grow, you will need more people and that means more jobs! It can be fun, exciting and rewarding. If you get it right, it can help you build a good life for you, your family and those who work for you.

## ARE THERE ANY DOWNSIDES?

Having your own business can also be risky, full of challenges and take up all your time. You will face tricky situations, have to make difficult decisions and, yes, it can be more flexible, but the responsibility stops with you. So, think carefully before you decide if this is for you.

## WHEN CAN I START A BUSINESS?

Good news, you can set up a business as a **sole trader** at any age! Of course, you must think how much time it will take and how you can fit that in with your education.

## HOW DO I SET UP AS A SOLE TRADER?

Choose your trading name, tell HMRC by registering online for 'self assessment' and that's it, you are in business! Being a sole trader is a great choice to start with. It's simple, cheap, quick and you can learn lots of stuff before you take on the responsibilities of being a company director.

BEFORE DECIDING YOUR BUSINESS NAME, CHECK ONLINE TO SEE IF THE DOMAIN NAME IS AVAILABLE OR IF THERE IS SOMEONE ELSE USING IT – YOU DON'T WANT TO HAVE TO CHANGE IT AFTER YOU'VE HAD PACKAGING PRINTED!

## WHEN CAN I SET UP MY OWN COMPANY?

At 16 you can set up your own company, but there is a lot of stuff you will struggle with because you can't enter into a binding contract or open a business bank account, so it's a good idea to wait until you are at least 18, or find someone to join you as a company director who is 18 or over.

## WHAT IS THE DIFFERENCE BETWEEN BEING SELF-EMPLOYED AND A SOLE TRADER?

They are kind of the same thing – they both mean that you are responsible for working out and paying your own tax (self assessment). A **sole trader** describes the type of business you are and **self-employed** says you are working for yourself.

AS SOON AS YOU START SELLING STUFF REGULARLY AND TELLING PEOPLE ABOUT YOUR BUSINESS, HMRC SEES YOU AS A SOLE TRADER, SO YOU MUST REGISTER WITH THEM WITHIN THREE MONTHS, OR YOU PAY A PENALTY.

## WHAT IF I WANT TO SET UP A BUSINESS WITH A FRIEND?

It's the same as a sole trader, except there's more than one of you. You must tell HMRC who is responsible for the business records and tax returns (the 'nominated person'). It is also a good idea to have a simple agreement between you, about who owns what, what each of you does, etc. To help save misunderstandings and fall outs later!

KEEP GOOD RECORDS OF EARNINGS AND SPENDING AS YOU GO, OR YOU'LL GET MUDDLED WHEN YOU FILL OUT YOUR TAX RETURNS!

## WHAT IS A BUSINESS PLAN?

It is like a map – it takes you from where you are to where you want your business to be. It says what your business is, why it is needed, where it is going and what you will need to get there. It will also answer the question: Why will my business succeed?

## WHY DO I NEED A BUSINESS PLAN?

A bit like a budget, you will want a business plan because it makes you think hard about what you want to do and helps you stay in control. It's mainly for you, but as your business gets bigger you might need it to borrow money or ask people to invest. They are going to want to see that you know where your business is going and how you are going to do it!

## HOW DO I MAKE A BUSINESS PLAN?

It can be really simple – the best ones are! The big thing is the thinking time you put in. You can dream a bit here, some of the huge names we all know today came from dreams. They make you imagine what your business can be and you can't be what you can't imagine! To help get started, *see page 134.*

## BUILD YOUR BUSINESS PLAN

Start by writing down what your business is, why it is needed and what you want it to be: **your goals**.

Now answer these questions:

- **How** will it make money?

- **Who** are you going to sell to? (Your **market**.)

- How are they going to know about you? (**Marketing**.)

- Why is your business better than anything else out there? (**Competitive advantage**.)

- What **skills** are needed and when? (Include your own skills.)

- **What else** do you need? (Office, computer, phones, etc.)

Now you need to know how much all this will cost and of course how much money will be coming in and when. Guess what? You are going to need a budget! *See page 62* for more info on budgets.

## I'VE REGISTERED MY BUSINESS, NOW WHAT?

Get started! You need to organise the stuff needed to carry out your business (**operations**), e.g. . . .

- Finding somewhere to work and buying the equipment you need.

- Finding suppliers if you are selling stuff.

- Understanding the laws and taxes for your business.

- Setting up your processes, such as how you keep your money records or accounts.

- Making sure you have enough money to pay for everything.

## WHAT TAXES DO I HAVE TO PAY?

Income tax and National Insurance. If you're really successful and your income hits an amount the government sets, called the VAT threshold, you must tell HMRC and register to pay VAT.

## HOW DOES VAT WORK?

You add VAT on to the price that you sell for. Your customers pay it and at the end of a period ('quarter'), you will hand that money to HMRC. Yep, you become a tax collector! The good news is that if you are VAT registered, you can get any VAT back you pay on the stuff you buy for your business!

## WHAT IS LOSS?

If you have spent more than your income, then that is a loss (called **net loss**).

## WHAT IS PROFIT?

Profit is how much money is left after you have paid ALL your business costs (called **net profit**).

## IS THERE A DIFFERENCE BETWEEN NET PROFIT AND GROSS PROFIT?

Yes, quite a big one! If I buy a mug for £2 and sell it for £4, then my gross profit is £2, because that's the money I made directly on the mug. BUT, there are lots of other costs involved in running the business (marketing, staff, etc.) and these are called **overheads**. Net profit takes all costs into account, not just the cost of the mug. This is sometimes called 'the bottom line', because in accounts, that is exactly where it is!

## WHAT IS A BALANCE SHEET?

This balances what you own (assets) on one side and what you owe (**liabilities**) on the other. If you own more than you owe, what is left belongs to the company or shareholders (**equity**). If you owe more than you own, you could be in trouble.

> YOU CAN MAKE A GOOD PROFIT
> BUT RUN OUT OF MONEY,
> SO KEEPING AN EYE ON BOTH
> IS VERY IMPORTANT.

## WHAT IS THE DIFFERENCE BETWEEN CASHFLOW AND PROFIT?

**Cashflow** shows when money comes in and goes out of your business, which is very different to profit. Let's see why that matters . . .

Imagine you have £150. It costs you £50 to run your business every month. You have found some gorgeous decorations you want to sell, so you buy them for £150 in October and sell ALL of them two months later in December for £300. That's twice as much as you paid for them – hurrah! Or is it? Can you spot the problem?

Answer: It costs £100 to run your business between October and December, so you have no money left to pay your bills until you make your profit in December and if you can't borrow any money, that could be a disaster!

# INTERVIEW WITH
# GARY NEVILLE

Football commentator and former football player, co-owner of Salford City football club and business owner

## WHAT MADE YOU GO INTO BUSINESS?

Initially, it was my interest and love of property and real estate. Through doing up my own houses I got the bug and I wanted to do it more and more. I bought a couple of farms in Bolton (where I lived) that I gained planning permission on for 10–12 houses and then turned that into a business.

## HOW DO YOU KNOW A BUSINESS WILL WORK?

When you go into business, there is always an element of not being sure that it will work. However, the fundamentals need to be right – the partner, the product, the people, the location, the funding, the idea and the concept. If these key things aren't right at the beginning, it's very difficult to make it work. For me, the most important element is the people; the quality and the ethos of the people, their attitude, their spirit and their desire to really go down a long, hard road together. Business doesn't come easy!

## HOW DO YOU DEAL WITH SETBACKS?

I've had few setbacks within my businesses where I've had to close them down. If a business isn't right, close it down ASAP. Don't prolong it. There is a balance between something that's not working vs persistence and staying with it and making it work. It's that judgement call that you only learn through experience.

## BEST PIECE OF ADVICE YOU'VE BEEN GIVEN?

My Dad told me to work as hard as I possibly could every single day and not give in, have no regrets and never look back on something and wish I could have done more. These are the principles and values that I've lived by through my career and life, and they've always stood me in pretty good stead.

## WHAT ARE YOUR TOP THREE TIPS?

**1.** Get the right team and people around you.
**2.** Be knowledgeable and passionate about the sector.
**3.** Be brave.

## WHAT IF MY BUSINESS DOESN'T WORK?

If your business isn't working, find out why. Be honest with yourself because you may be causing some of the problems! If you think changing things will fix the business, then make the changes and keep going, but if it is a problem you can't work out or fix, then it might be time to stop and think of something else!

## HOW DO I AVOID MAKING MISTAKES?

It's not about avoiding mistakes, because we all make and learn from them, it's about making sure your mistakes don't cause a business catastrophe and you do that by planning, listening to advice and weighing up risks.

IN BUSINESS YOU DON'T HAVE TO GET EVERYTHING RIGHT — JUST MORE RIGHT THAN WRONG.

IF YOU ARE NOT MAKING MISTAKES, THEN YOU ARE NOT PUSHING HARD ENOUGH.

## WHEN BUSINESS GOES WRONG

I had a business importing beautiful Italian homeware. It was going really well until the shops started buying direct instead of coming through me. The business failed leaving me £3,000 in debt, but I learnt valuable lessons and used them to make sure I didn't make the same mistakes again. Although I had a contract, I decided not to waste my time and more money taking them to court. Instead, I looked for another opportunity.

**NEARLY EVERY SUCCESSFUL ENTREPRENEUR I KNOW HAS FAILED AT SOME POINT.**

IT'S NOT THE FAILURE BUT HOW YOU DEAL WITH IT THAT MATTERS.

Thanks for reading the book – I hope you enjoyed it and now feel more confident with finance. Always remember to make your money work for you and use the tools you have learned to build a happy and healthy relationship with money.

**KNOWLEDGE IS POWER, SO KEEP LEARNING EVERY DAY.**

# INDEX

apprenticeships 42

automatic payments 106

balance sheets 136

banknotes 10, 11, 13, 14

banks 69, 71, 72, 76, 77
online 78–81

bartering 10

Bartlett, Steven 126, 128–129

benefits 83

bills 104, 105, 106

bitcoin 25, 26, 28, 29

bonds 52

borrowing 16, 17, 114–123

budgets 62–67, 96–97, 106

building societies 72

business
mistakes 138–139
plans 133–134
starting a 36, 126–127, 130–131

buy now, pay later 116

careers 42

cash 10, 14, 21

Chilton, Beth 89

coins 10, 12, 14, 21

counterfeits 14, 15

cover letters 35

credit cards 24, 101, 115, 121, 122

credit scores 107, 120

credit unions 116

cryptocurrencies 24–29

CVs 34, 35

currency 22, 23

debit cards 121

debt 117, 122–124

deposits 107, 108, 111

digital money 24

direct debits 106

eco-friendly 13, 29

economy 14, 54–56

Ellis-Bextor, Sophie 38–39

exchange rate 23

fiat money 11

fundraising 37

gold standard 11

Gross Domestic Product (GDP) 55, 56

happiness 30

hire purchase (HP) 115

**inflation** 16–17, 20, 21

**insurance** 83, 101–103

**interest**
  loans 114, 119, 122
  mortgages 110
  rates 17, 71
  savings 68, 71, 74

**investing** 75

**Jefferies, Andy** 62, 67

**jobs, finding** 32–34

**loans** 110, 114,
  117–119, 122

**Lycett, Joe** 43, 44–45

**money laundering** 27

**money mules** 26, 27

**mortgages** 110

**National Debt** 53

**National Insurance** 48

**negotiating** 94

**Neville, Gary** 138–139

**offshore accounts** 84

**overdrafts** 72, 114

**payslips** 40–41

**peer-to-peer lending**
  116

**pensions** 82

**prepaid cards** 121

**recession** 56

**rent** 104–105, 107–109

**salaries** *see* wages

**saving** 21, 30
  accounts 68, 70
  interest rates 17

**scams** 26, 27, 81

**self-employed** 132

**Shah, Anusha** 91

**shopping** 88, 90,
  92–100

**sole trader** 131, 132

**standing orders** 106

**Steele, Tanya** 97

**Styles, Harry** 33

**supply and demand** 18,
  23, 26, 46

**Swift, Taylor** 33

**tax returns** 132

**taxes** 45, 48–51, 84,
  135

**transaction fees** 72

**value** 11, 26, 75, 92,
  94, 102

**VAT** 48, 135

**volunteering** 37

**wages** 46–47

**zero-hours contracts**
  47